EMPANADAS

THE HAND-HELD PIES OF LATIN AMERICA

★ SANDRA A. GUTIERREZ ★  PHOTOGRAPHS BY TINA RUPP

STEWART, TABORI & CHANG, NEW YORK

CONTENTS

INTRODUCTION	**5**
THE EMPANADA KITCHEN & PANTRY	**11**
WITHIN THE CRUST	**17**
Cooked Flank Steak	18
Poached Chicken	19
EMPANADA DOUGH	**20**
Masa Dough	24
Cornmeal Dough	26
Cornmeal and Cassava Dough	27
Cassava or Yuca Dough	28
Master Dough	29
Bread Dough	30
Salteña Dough	32
Pastéis Dough	33
Flaky Dough	34
Sweet Plantain Dough	35
VEGETABLE, NUT & CHEESE EMPANADAS	**36**
Spicy Potato and Peanut Empanadas	38
Cheesy Spinach Empanadas	41
Corn and Spanish Smoked Paprika Turnovers	44
Roquefort and Walnut Mini Pies	46
Cheese and Loroco Masa Pies	49
Black Bean and Cheese "Domino" Pies	52
Flaky Hearts of Palm Pillows	55
Fried Cassava and Cheese Turnovers	58
Light-as-Air Onion and Cheese Pies	61
BEEF & PORK EMPANADAS	**64**
Hand-Cut Beef, Egg, and Green Onion Empanadas	66
Famous Beef, Raisin, and Olive Hand Pies	69
Golden and Juicy Beef and Potato Pies	72
Sweet Plantain and Beef Turnovers	75
Beef and Dried Chile Masa Pies	78
Cumin Shredded Beef Empanadas	81
Ravioli-Shaped Pies with Stir-Fried Beef, Onions, and Peppers	84
Flaky Ground Beef and Herb Pillows	87

Crispy Cassava and Beef Empanadas 90

Sugar-Coated Pork and Raisin Turnovers 93

Sweet and Savory Pork Pies 96

Classic Ham and Cheese Pockets 98

Chorizo and Potato Pies with Tomatillo Salsa 101

CHICKEN EMPANADAS 104

Creamy Chicken and Mushroom Empanadas 106

Chicken Masa Pies with Lettuce and Radishes 110

Sweet and Savory Chicken, Roasted Red Pepper, and Olive Pies 113

Chicken Pies with Pecan and Yellow Pepper Sauce 116

Stewed Chicken and Annatto Corn Empanadas 119

Green Tomatillo Chicken Stew Empanadas 122

Golden Chicken, Potato, and Green Pea Pies 125

FISH & SEAFOOD EMPANADAS 128

Shrimp and Tomato Stew Flaky Pillows 130

Creamy Tuna and Roasted Red Pepper Pies 133

Maria José's Tuna, Jalapeño, and Tomato Turnovers 136

Cod and Potato Turnovers with Stewed Tomatoes and Olives 139

DESSERT EMPANADAS 142

Caramel-Apple Pies 144

Candied Pineapple Pies 148

Banana Pastries Coated with Sugar and Cinnamon 151

Guava and Cream Cheese Pastries 154

Jam and Cream Cheese Mini Pies 157

SALSAS 160

Knife-Cut Parsley Sauce 162

Red Pepper Salsa 164

Creamy Peanut Sauce with Toppings 165

Avocado Salsa 167

Mango and Avocado Salsa 168

Dried Chile, Bell Pepper, and Tomato Sauce 169

Yellow Pepper Aioli 170

Raw Tomatillo Salsa 171

SOURCES 172

INDEX 173

ACKNOWLEDGMENTS 176

INTRODUCTION

★ THE STORY OF THE EMPANADA: A JOURNEY ★

I've always been a curious person. I love boxes, baskets, and anything that can hide treasures within. When I hold an unopened box in my hand I get the same feeling that I experience when I hold an empanada for the first time: fascination and a curiosity to discover what scrumptious surprises lie hidden inside. It's this curiosity that has made it so fascinating for me to research the history of food. It's what leads me to want to learn why we eat what we eat, where our food comes from, and how it has evolved over time. After sleuthing like a detective and finding some answers, I always feel compelled to guess where food will go next. Few stories enthrall me more than the evolution of the empanada, because we can trace it back to ancient times but it continues to evolve today.

AT THE BEGINNING

The name *empanada* derives from the Latin *in panis,* or "in bread." In Spanish, *empanar* means "to encase in bread," and empanadas are hand-held pockets stuffed with a marvelous array of fillings. Many cultures have a tradition of hand-held pies: Italy has calzones, Jamaica has patties, India has samosas, and Britain has pasties. Nevertheless, no other culture has a larger compendium of hand-held pies than Latin America.

Empanadas have an early history wrapped in wars and conquests. The very first empanadas most likely originated in Persia, where travelers and laborers alike turned to this humble food for comfort and nourishment in ancient times. In fact, we can trace the origins of hand-held pies as far back as the year 250 BCE, and to the territory that is modern-day Iran. In order to preserve foods, the Persians used to encase fillings in rustic dough. Not only did the dough keep the fillings from spoiling, but it also made them highly portable. The dough itself was not necessarily meant to be eaten at first, although it morphed into an edible case. These moveable meals were ideal for nomadic cultures, shepherds, and for the legions of soldiers who traveled constantly in their quest to expand the Muslim empire. Today, in the Middle East, we can still find *fatays* or *esfiha* (made with wheat flour and filled with lamb), which are perhaps the closest relatives of the first filled pastries.

Empanadas appeared wherever the Ottoman Empire left its imprint and began to be known under different names in the many countries the Ottomans conquered. Once they found their way into Spain's territories, however, all of these bread-encrusted meals became known in the Spanish language simply as "empanadas." And by the time the Muslims were expelled from Spain in the 1400s, these hand-held pies had spread throughout Europe. For example, ancient Romans encased sheep's milk cheese in thin sheets of pastry similar to phyllo dough.

EMPANADAS TO GO

Empanadas have always been lauded for their portable characteristics, and as convenient on-the-go sustenance the empanada was a favorite of pilgrims. Ancient stone sculptures in the city of Santiago de Compostela in Galicia, Spain, illustrate scenes of pilgrims in search of Saint James's tomb, carrying empanadas for their long expeditions.

Being tantalizingly delicious and portable is precisely why empanadas were able to spread around the world. Shortly after the Ottoman Empire fell, the Spanish Empire began its global expansion, and consequently the territory occupied by empanadas also spread. Wherever the *conquistadores* went, so did these edible parcels. The first empanadas arrived in the Americas in the early 1500s. The most common fillings consisted of minced lamb, studded with raisins and seasoned with spices in the Arab style; fish, as was customary in Galicia; and cheese, as was traditional in some Middle Eastern and Mediterranean cultures. To this day, the most frequently found empanadas in the Latin American landscape still feature fillings that derived from those dating back to medieval times— most particularly from the Moorish mishmash of meat, onions, dried fruits, eggs, and spices.

What happened next was numerically astonishing, as each Latin American country began to multiply empanada recipes exponentially, giving these their own twists and replacing the traditional ingredients with those native to each area. By now, each country and region within each country offers a plethora of permutations. So, while the sixteenth century may have been when hand-held pies entered the culinary landscape of Latin America, the twenty-first century marks the period when empanadas have reached the zenith of popularity. Today, empanadas are more in vogue than ever before.

EMPANADAS TODAY

Empanadas are still as portable today as they were centuries ago, and this makes them ideal for modern times when eating on the go is the norm. In Latin America, children often find empanadas lovingly tucked into their lunchboxes, and busy people carry boxes filled with empanadas home after work to set up for impromptu entertaining. In fact, you will find empanadas—and not tortillas, which are not found past Central America as they are replaced by other flatbreads such as *arepas* and *cachapas*—on tables from Mexico all the way to Argentina.

Empanadas in modern-day Latin America are enjoyed in restaurants, sold by street food vendors, and prepared by home cooks alike. Some are sold by merchants near sports stadiums or bus terminals, such as the Guatemalan peanut and chocolate empanadas. Other empanadas are solely found in the vicinity of churches on Sunday mornings, such as the Colombian *empanadas de parroquia* or "parish empanadas," filled with beef and potatoes. Another famous example of these empanadas is called *vaticana* ("from the Vatican"), filled solely with potatoes, which are sold in the porticos and plazas of churches in Medellín. In fact, it is said that many churches in Colombia have been built and restored thanks to empanada bake sales. Since empanadas are not expensive to make, selling them is often a great means to raise funds.

Empanadas also have an economic role in the lives of many Latin American home cooks (particularly women), who depend on selling empanadas to sustain their families. Most of the street vendors who sell empanadas are widows, single mothers, or low-income women who use the money provided by their sales to raise their children and to help their families subsist.

Some empanadas are traditionally eaten only during certain holidays, such as the *empanadas Gallegas* stuffed with tuna, which make their appearance every year during the Lenten season throughout the entire Latin American continent. Others, such as the *pastelitos de membrillo* ("quince empanadas"), are commonly eaten mid-afternoon with a cup of coffee or tea in Argentina as everyday fare. Empanadas are so central to Latin American culture that many places hold entire festivals around them (for example, the Fiesta de la Empanada in Concón, Chile, and the many different *fiestas de la Salteña* held from Salta, Argentina, to Cochabamba, Bolivia).

SOMETHING FOR EVERY PALATE

Modern-day Latin American empanadas are stuffed with everything from corn, cheese, meat, fowl, seafood, vegetables, herbs, and fruits to caramels (called *manjares*) and jams, depending on which one of the twenty-one countries that we call Latin America you happen to be in. Latin American empanadas also go by different names: *dobladas, salteñas, pastéis, rellenitos, molotes,* and *pasteles,* among them. Some have dry fillings and others, like the Bolivian *salteñas*, are often so juicy that you need a spoon to eat them. Some are spicy, while others are not; some are eaten alone, while others are doused with sauces. Some empanadas are meant to be eaten at room temperature, such as those stuffed with rice pudding or custards, while others must always be enjoyed piping hot, as is the case with most of the fried empanadas.

Perhaps the most famous Latin American empanadas are those that feature fillings made of beef, raisins, and olives— a combination that originated with the Moors and one that is found from Cuba all the way to Argentina. In Argentina alone, where beef empanadas are particularly popular, this kind of empanada varies by region. In the northern region of Tucumán, for example, beef empanadas always feature a moist filling made with knife-cut beef, while those that hail from Córdoba feature potato in the filling and are always coated with sugar. Both are beef empanadas, but each one has its own characteristics. Indeed, every Latin American country features at least one variation of the classic beef empanada. However, beef empanadas are only the beginning.

There are as many versions of empanadas as there are cooks. Making an all-encompassing compendium of empanadas, therefore, is an impossible task. However, here you'll find empanadas featuring fillings that represent the many cultures that have helped to shape the individual cuisines of Latin America. I offer you, for example, a contemporary Peruvian empanada featuring a modern filling of the Spanish-influenced *ají de gallina* (a stew of pulled chicken in a spicy nut and cheese sauce), and others stuffed with French-inspired fillings made with béchamel sauce and vegetables. Still others are filled with the Asian-inspired beef stir-fry called *lomo saltado*, which is seasoned with soy sauce. A far departure from the first empanadas to reach the New World, these are native interpretations using modern cooking techniques and fused flavors of the cultures that collided in the American territory, after centuries of culinary history and amalgamation.

NOT ALL EMPANADAS ARE CREATED EQUAL

In addition to the huge variety of fillings and flavors, the shapes, sizes, textures, types of dough, and methods of preparation vary widely. Some empanadas are round, some look like small torpedoes or footballs, and others are shaped like half-moons. You'll find them in all sizes: Some are tiny and meant to be enjoyed for a midday snack, while others are very large and meant to take the place of an entire meal. Some empanadas are sealed decoratively, while others feature simple crimped edges, and yet others are square and folded like envelopes. Some are soft, while others are crispy; some empanadas are fried, while others are grilled or baked.

In Brazil, empanadas are made with flaky pastry dough, while Colombians use precooked cornmeal to encase theirs. In Mexico and Central America, you'll find empanada dough made with nixtamalized corn masa, and in South America, you'll find them made with cassava dough.

HOMEMADE AND STOREBOUGHT

Some empanada recipes are carefully guarded by families and many are passed along generationally. Most recipes are born of happenstance, when ingredients left over from other meals become the fillings used in making empanadas. However, those who don't make their own empanadas can always count on professional bakers. There are bakeries all over Latin America that specialize in these stuffed bread parcels, and many become famous for their own variety of empanadas.

I have clear recollections of shopping at my neighborhood's bakery in Guatemala City, where my mother would place advance orders for their pastries. If I was well behaved, I could usually cajole my mother into rewarding me with one of the flaky empanadas stuffed with savory beef sitting behind the glass stand. Just as that bakery was known for a particular kind of beef empanada, thousands of small mom-and-pop–owned bakeries around the Americas specialize in their own recipes.

In Latin America, it's not uncommon for home cooks to buy empanadas to serve as appetizers (known also as *boquitas, aperitivos, botanas, las onces, pasabocas,* or *pasapalos,* depending on what country you're in) with a drink or a glass of wine before a late Sunday lunch or weeknight supper. Empanadas can be—and, in fact, are—enjoyed at any time of the day.

YES, REAL MEN EAT EMPANADAS

If you don't believe me, ask South American men. Argentina, Chile, Bolivia, and Uruguay make up the area of Latin America where empanadas are almost ritualistic. In Latin America, empanadas break through social class, gender, and occasion. Rich and poor eat them just the same, and they're equally at home at a high society wedding where they're served with champagne as they are every afternoon when laborers meet in their *barrio* ("neighborhood") cafés and enjoy them alongside a cup of *yerba mate* or *café con leche*.

THE EVOLUTION CONTINUES

It used to be that one bite into an empanada could help us taste the past, but today it can also predict future culinary trends. New empanada creations are born every day, limited only by the curiosity of deft cooks who wish to stretch a few ingredients—perhaps last night's leftovers, or bits and pieces that alone don't amount to much but that in combination offer a succulent mishmash of flavors—and preserve them inside a crust. Each empanada—whether it is a traditional kind or a new interpretation—is a parcel of culinary idiosyncrasy and a gift to the palate.

By now, even most North American children have encountered one form of hand-held pie or another—perhaps called by a different name, such as "pocket" or "patty." However, no matter the name, empanadas have continued to be an important aspect of our foodways. And today, as the mass immigration of millions of Latin Americans affects other areas of the world, empanadas are experiencing a renaissance in other cultures. Take Paris—considered by so many to be the ultimate culinary Mecca—where food stores, such as Buena Onda, specialize in

Argentinean empanadas. Also in Paris, there are eateries, such as Clasico Argentino, that offer both sit-down service and home delivery of empanadas to their customers throughout the City of Lights. In Frankfurt, Germany, you can purchase a good variety of empanadas, including those at Empanadiso. And in Berlin, there are also many places to purchase empanadas including Marques, Restaurant La Batea, Parakas, and Torito Latino. Even in Toronto, Canada (where I lived for nine years), you can purchase Chilean empanadas in the city's famous Kensington Market. Empanadas are no longer contained in a geographic bubble.

As long as street food, portable meals, and homemade comfort cooking remain popular, we can expect that the love affair with empanadas will grow and so will the list of new recipes. And as more and more Latin Americans migrate to other parts of the world, intermarry, and continue to change the foodways of their new homes, the popularity of empanadas will continue to soar. Visit Manhattan, Chicago, or Los Angeles, and you'll find plenty of eateries serving empanadas. Even in smaller cities (such as Charlottesville, Virginia, and Durham, North Carolina, where I live), empanada cafés are starting to become popular.

ABOUT THIS BOOK

I believe that empanadas are at the backbone of Latin America, uniting peoples of different cultures. Therefore, I wrote this book as a guide to some of the most recognized authentic Latin American empanadas. The recipes I collected here are fun and varied, and they span from Mexico all the way down to Brazil. They are my favorites, tried and tested to be delicious.

My goal is to provide you with practical recipes that are easy to follow and that work every time. Since empanada recipes have been traditionally passed down from one generation to the next, and since we don't all have a Latin mother or grandmother standing with us in the kitchen, I hope that you will feel as though I'm there, next to you, guiding you in a friendly manner, as you learn to make these individual pastries. My recipes fit

the modern cook's kitchen. I've written them so that you can divide your tasks into smaller ones that take less time. I give you basic techniques and offer the use of modern appliances available in most kitchens, in hopes that you will be able to make empanadas often and with the least possible exertion.

In these pages, you'll find information on how to shape empanadas with ease, when to make the fillings (always before the dough), and how to reheat them. You'll also find an entire chapter on the best sauces to pair with these empanadas.

All of the recipes that you'll find in this book are authentic to Latin America, and each will tell you where a particular empanada is from. Although all of the empanadas in this book (e.g., the *salteñas* and the *pastéis*) are traditionally made with different, specific kinds of homemade dough, you can adapt these recipes to your own purposes and select a different dough to encase a particular filling. For instance, recipes can be made gluten-free by selecting a dough made with masa, plantain, or cornmeal instead of flour. And to save time, most fillings may be wrapped in store-bought empanada discs found in the freezer section of many Latin American stores and large grocery store chains around the world.

Spend an afternoon or two crafting these individual pies and you can have delicious food on hand for weeks to come, if you would prefer to freeze them for later consumption; follow the instructions on how to freeze each kind, which I offer you at the end of each recipe.

Making empanadas is a culinary tradition worth keeping and building upon, and it is my hope that this book will open up the world of authentic Latin American empanadas for you, and that you will start making them at home and sharing them with others. I hope, too, that you will be inspired to create new interpretations that include your favorite flavors. The possibilities are endless: BLT empanadas, macaroni and cheese empanadas, pizza pies, and peanut butter and jelly empanaditas, to name just a few. Let your imagination and your palate guide you. After all, everything tastes better when wrapped in a crust!

THE EMPANADA KITCHEN & PANTRY

+++

★ ESSENTIAL EQUIPMENT AND INGREDIENTS ★

Most of what you'll need to make empanadas is probably already housed in your kitchen, so chances are you won't have to invest in much (if any) special equipment. Some of the ingredients you'll need, however, may be new to you. Use this list, sequenced roughly in order of importance, as your guide for interpreting those ingredients and tools that you need to familiarize yourself with before you set out to conquer the craft of empanada making.

★ ★ ★ EQUIPMENT ★ ★ ★

TORTILLA PRESS

I use a tortilla press to shape most of the empanada wrappers in this book. You can find tortilla presses online and in many Latino stores. For the most part, they're inexpensive; on average they cost around $20. Some are made out of wood, but the majority of them are made out of cast iron. Most are 6½ to 7 inches (about 17 cm) in diameter. Larger ones can measure 10 inches (25 cm) in diameter. Most are round, but some are square. The shape or material they're made of won't make a difference in a recipe, but you will need one that is at least 6½ inches (about 17 cm) wide. If you don't feel like investing in one, use a rolling pin instead. You must always line a tortilla press with a plastic bag (zip-top freezer bags cut open on three sides like a book work great) or with parchment paper so that the dough won't stick to the surface when you press it.

KITCHEN SCALE

I love my kitchen scale and use it a lot. When it comes to baking, I find that weight measurements yield better results than volume measurements (particularly when it comes to dividing dough into exact portions so that all of the empanadas can be the same size in each batch). All of the dough recipes in the book have been measured both ways, for your convenience. However, if you can, buy a good kitchen scale.

ZIP-TOP PLASTIC FREEZER BAGS

You will use these to line the tortilla press each time you flatten out dough. They're also useful in protecting the surface of your kitchen scale when you measure out ingredients. You'll also need plenty of these if you're freezing large batches of empanadas.

SHARP KITCHEN SCISSORS

These will come in handy every time you need to cut strings off ingredients, as well as to cut open the bags used to line your tortilla press.

RULER

Why guess the length and diameter of empanada discs when you can measure them quickly? I have a stainless-steel ruler that can go directly into my dishwasher after it's used.

DUTCH OVEN

I depend on my enamel-coated Dutch ovens when I fry my empanadas because they're tall enough that the splatter is minimal, and they keep the oil at a stable temperature during frying. A 5- or 6-quart (4.7- or 5.7-L) size works well.

DEEP-FRYING THERMOMETER

This will be important to help you determine the right temperature of oil before and during frying. Make sure it is a thermometer that is intended for deep-fat frying.

DEEP-FAT FRYER

I must confess that I don't own one, but if you have one, you'll want to use it to fry larger batches of empanadas. Make sure to follow the manufacturer's instructions.

CAST-IRON SKILLET

Mine is a sturdy skillet from the Lodge Cast Iron company in

Tennessee. It's so useful whenever I need to char vegetables for salsas, and to shallow-fry small batches of tiny empanadas.

BAKING SHEETS OR HALF-SHEET PANS

You'll need several heavy-duty sheet pans with rimmed sides in order to bake the empanadas in this book. These are also great to place the empanadas as you shape them, to chill the empanadas that must be refrigerated before they can be cooked (to set up their shape), and to freeze them.

PARCHMENT PAPER

Parchment paper is silicone-coated baking paper that prevents food from sticking to baking sheets; it withstands pretty high temperatures in the oven without burning. It's also ideal when cut into small squares to divide raw empanada dough discs so that they don't stick together. I prefer the unbleached kind, but either one works fine. I keep several rolls of this paper in my kitchen at all times. It can be reused several times before you need to discard it. Do not substitute waxed paper unless you want your food to taste like crayon (as the wax melts and sticks to the food) and the paper to ignite in the oven.

COOLING RACKS

You'll need at least two metal cooling racks. These are great to cool the empanadas after baking them. Whenever I fry empanadas, I always set a cooling rack inside a high-rimmed baking sheet and place the empanadas there after frying them to drain the excess oil.

GRIDDLE

Some empanadas may be cooked on a griddle. You can use an electric griddle or, if you have a gas cooktop, use a flat and long griddle pan. Some griddles have a way to measure their temperature as well.

ASSORTED ROUND COOKIE CUTTERS

Having a collection of round cookie cutters in various sizes will be very helpful when making empanadas. Of course, you can do as Latin American cooks have done for centuries and use round plates (or glasses) to cut discs of different sizes too.

STURDY ROLLING PIN

Every cook has a favorite rolling pin, but I'm partial to the tapered wooden (French) pins because they make rolling the dough a bit easier by allowing you to apply pressure throughout the pin, thus producing more evenly thinned-out dough.

PASTRY CUTTER

You'll need one whenever square-shaped empanada dough is called for, such as for the Brazilian *pastéis* in this book.

MEASURING CUPS

No, they're not created equal. Glass measuring cups are good only for liquids. You'll need a set to measure the solid ingredients (such as flours and sugar) too.

MEASURING SPOONS

A reliable set of measuring spoons will help you so you don't have to guess. This is particularly important when making dough, which requires measuring precise amounts.

POTATO MASHER

It will come in handy when pureeing plantains and cassava (yuca) for the empanadas in this book.

FOOD PROCESSOR

Most of the dough recipes in this book are made entirely by hand, but there are a few exceptions, for which a food processor is preferred. A food processor will also help you to pulverize some of the beef fillings and other ingredients.

BLENDER

Without a doubt, it is one of the most hardworking appliances in the Latin American kitchen. Use it to make sauces and to fully puree ingredients as called for in this book.

★ ★ ★ INGREDIENTS ★ ★ ★

JALAPEÑO PEPPERS

CILANTRO & CILANTRO FLOWERS

AJÍES CACHUCHAS

POBLANO PEPPERS

TOMATILLOS

ALL-PURPOSE FLOUR

I prefer the unbleached kind. If you buy it in bulk, like me, keep it in your freezer for up to two years. Bring it back to room temperature before using.

MASA HARINA AND MASAREPA

It is important to make a distinction between the two types of corn flour that you will need to make the empanadas in this book, because you cannot substitute one corn flour for the other, if you want your empanadas to be authentic to their country of origin.

Masa harina is the dried corn flour that you'll use to make many of the Mexican and Central American recipes in this book. The corn is treated with calcium hydroxide (known as *cal* in Spanish), has its hulls slipped, and then it's dried.

The dried corn, also known as hominy, is then ground to a meal that only needs the addition of water to become masa. There are many brands of masa harina out there, but I recommend using the two most popular brands available: Maseca or Torti Masa. The bags sometimes say "Instant Corn Masa Flour." This nixtamalized corn masa is not used in South America.

Harina pan or masarepa is a type of cornmeal in which the corn is dried and ground before it is precooked without any addition of chemicals (i.e., no *cal*). It is used in Colombia and Venezuela. It comes in two colors: white and yellow. Either one will work for the recipes in this book. Two very popular brands are Goya and P.A.N. Please be advised that regular cornmeal cannot be substituted for *masarepa*, since regular cornmeal has not been treated in the same manner.

FINE SEA SALT

It dissolves easily in recipes and has a clean taste that doesn't overpower the other ingredients.

LARD OR TALLOW

In Latin America, two different kinds of rendered animal fat are used in baking: pork lard (*manteca de cerdo*) and beef tallow (*grasa de pella*). In South American countries such as Chile and Argentina, beef tallow is preferred, although cooks use it interchangeably with lard. Finding rendered beef tallow is very difficult and you'll probably have to render it yourself. Unlike lard, tallow turns rancid quickly after it's been rendered. For these reasons, I will often suggest that you stick with lard.

As maligned as fat has been in our modern culture, it is still the best vehicle for flavor. Lard plays an important role in the making of empanadas because it produces tender crusts. It melts at a slower rate than butter when exposed to heat, and this makes for flakier pastries. Even though you can always substitute vegetable shortening for lard in the recipes in this book (perfect for vegetarians), know that authentic empanadas

will most often be made with lard. In the United States and abroad, many grocery stores that cater to Latin American customers will sell tubs of golden rendered pork lard. I suggest you find a store near you that does this and buy it, freshly rendered, whenever you can. However, certainly you can rely on whatever is most convenient for you, whether it is vegetable shortening; store-bought, freshly rendered lard; or homemade lard or tallow. But stay away from the white, hydrogenated lard found in most supermarkets; it's both unhealthy and has been stripped of flavor.

To produce tallow, you must start with beef fat (called suet) that comes from the fatty tissue surrounding the kidneys or loin of the steer (ask your butcher to reserve it for you). For lard, you must select the pork belly or fatback (leaf lard) from the pig, or random pieces of fat from the pig. Leaf lard produces milky-white fat, while the other produces golden, nutty lard. Both are equally fine to use in the recipes in this book. The crispy pieces left after rendering the fat are known as *chicharrones* or cracklings; use or discard, as you please. When chilled, lard and tallow will solidify, making them easy to measure for the recipes in this book.

How to Render Tallow and Lard: Cut the fat into small pieces and place it in a heavy (preferably enameled, cast-iron) pot. Turn the heat on to low and cook slowly, uncovered, until the fat melts away and is separated from any pieces of meat. Strain the fat through a fine mesh strainer and transfer it to clean containers with lids. Store lard in the refrigerator for up to 6 months (tallow for 3 days) or in the freezer, for up to 1 year (tallow for 1 month).

UNSALTED BUTTER

Unsalted butter allows you to add salt to taste in your recipes.

CREAM CHEESE

Full-fat cream cheese is necessary for the recipes in this book. Don't substitute with any other.

MANGO

PLANTAINS

YUCA

CASSAVA OR YUCA

This tuber is available frozen and ready to cook in many Latin American *tiendas* and in the freezer section of many grocery stores in the United States. I prefer to buy it frozen because it's already been peeled and sectioned, saving me time in the kitchen.

CANNED REFRIED BEANS

A time-saver. Find your favorite brand and stick with that. My favorite is Ducal by Goya because the beans are smooth and nicely seasoned.

STORE-BOUGHT FROZEN EMPANADA DISCS

The empanada maker's best friends—simply thaw and fill, as these precut and premeasured empanada crusts are ready to

cook. You'll find them in the frozen section of many grocery stores and in most stores that cater to Latin Americans (see Sources, page 172).

The two most popular brands are La Fe and Goya. Some empanada discs have been colored with annatto to make them a dark golden (almost orange) color, while others are white. Use either kind, as the color won't affect the flavor of the final dish.

HARD-BOILED EGGS

These are commonly found in a wide range of empanadas and so it pays to be able to make them like a pro. To boil eggs, place the number of desired eggs in a pot large enough to hold them. Cover them by 2 inches (5 cm) with cold water. Bring the water to a rolling boil. Immediately remove the pot from the heat; cover the pot and let the eggs sit for 15 minutes. Drop the eggs into a bowl filled with iced water and let them cool completely. Peel and use as directed in each recipe.

ROASTED PEPPERS

These lend a smoky flavor to fillings like in the tuna empanadas on page 133. To make them, roast peppers directly over the flame of a gas stove, or grill or broil them until their skins are charred and blistered. Place them in a bowl; cover and let them steam for 20 minutes. Peel them by scraping the skins off with a sharp knife. Slice them in half and scrape the seeds off. You may also roast the peppers under a broiler; cut them in half (lengthwise) and place the peppers cut side down on a baking sheet.

GARLIC

LOROCO
FLOWER BUDS

ANCHO CHILES

ACHIOTE
(ANNATTO)

GUAJILLO
CHILES

MEXICAN
OREGANO

HONEY

MEMBRILLO

WITHIN THE CRUST

+++

★ FILLINGS AND COMMON INGREDIENTS ★

This chapter will help you to prepare the fillings for most of the beef and chicken empanadas in this book. These are also great stand-alone recipes that will come in handy in your kitchen. They would be delicious when simply served on a mound of rice and paired with a side salad. So whether you use these to make a particular empanada, or whether you just want good, clean Latin flavors on your table, these recipes are worthy of a special place in your culinary repertoire. I hope this chapter proves to be one that you will revisit with confidence, knowing that following these recipes and the general tips on fillings will ensure that your empanadas will be as authentic (and delicious!) as possible.

MAKING AND USING EMPANADA FILLINGS

★ Always make the fillings before you start the dough for the empanadas.

★ Chilling the fillings will make them much easier to handle, especially if they are moist. When moist fillings are properly chilled, they congeal, which makes them easier and neater to use. During the cooking process, moist fillings will warm up inside the dough and will become juicy once more.

★ The fillings must be heavily seasoned or else their flavor won't hold up to that of the dough used to encase them.

★ At first, you may have a hard time filling empanadas all the way through. It's best to start with less filling, so that the empanadas won't explode while cooking. You will get better at stuffing them as you go.

★ The fillings in this book have been carefully measured, so you shouldn't end up with much (if any) leftover filling; if you do, know that leftovers are great on their own, served on rice, or spread on a piece of toast.

★ The fillings will be very hot after the empanadas are cooked. Make sure to let the empanadas rest for several minutes before serving them.

★ Many of the empanadas in this book may be served at room temperature. It is imperative that the empanadas containing beef or dairy are not kept at room temperature for any longer than two hours after they are cooked. For this reason, if you need to keep the empanadas longer, either refrigerate and reheat them briefly, or freeze and reheat them before serving (according to the recipe).

COOKED FLANK STEAK

1 to 2 pounds (455 to 910 g) flank steak
(according to the recipe)

½ small white onion, halved

1 celery stalk (with leaves, preferred)

1 large or 2 small bay leaves

2 sprigs fresh thyme

1 large clove garlic

1 teaspoon fine sea salt

¼ teaspoon freshly ground black pepper

Flank steak is one of the most inexpensive cuts of beef and the preferred cut for most beef fillings used in Latin American empanadas. With a few exceptions, such as the Venezuelan empanadas, where the beef has to be seared before cooking, the steak is simply boiled in seasoned water until it is tender. Some cooks in South America barely blanch the beef before adding it to the rest of the ingredients, but others cook it through. Therefore, I've adapted this recipe, cooking the beef through until tender so that it works with most of the fillings in this book. Sometimes the recipe will call for the beef to be shredded, but other times it will require it to be finely diced. You can cook two or more steaks at a time, following the same method. Always reserve at least 1 cup (240 ml) of the cooking liquid, in case the empanada recipe calls for it.

+++

MAKES ABOUT 4 CUPS (960 ML)

Place the flank steak in a large pot. Pour in enough water to cover the steak by about 1½ inches (4 cm). Add the onion, celery, bay leaf, thyme, garlic, salt, and pepper. Bring the pot to a boil; cover, lower the heat, and simmer for 1½ hours, or until the beef is easily shredded with a fork.

Remove the steak from the pot, reserving 1 cup (240 ml) of the cooking liquid; set both aside. When the beef is cool enough to handle, remove any fat or sinew and slice it crosswise into thirds. Use your fingers to shred it into thin strands or chop it into a fine dice, according to the recipe; chill, covered, until ready to use.

> **NOTE:** If refrigerated, the steak will last, covered, for up to 2 days. To freeze it, cover the shredded beef with the cooking liquid just until submerged. Freeze it in containers for up to 3 months.

POACHED CHICKEN

There are many empanada recipes that start with cooked chicken. I encourage you to use organic and local chickens when you can. I select birds that include the neck and giblets so that I can benefit from their great flavor. Since chicken liver causes stock to become murky, I discard it or use it for other recipes. It is important to keep the liquid at a bare simmer while the chicken poaches so that the flesh remains moist and does not become stringy. Of course, you can use rotisserie chicken for any recipe in this book. However, if you cook your own, you'll find yourself armed with deeply flavored chicken and, as a bonus, luscious stock that can be used for preparing many other dishes.

+ +

MAKES ABOUT **4** CUPS (960 ML) COOKED WHITE MEAT, **2** CUPS (480 ML) COOKED DARK MEAT, AND **2** QUARTS (960 ML) BEAUTIFULLY SEASONED STOCK

Remove the giblets and neck from the cavity of the bird; discard the liver (or reserve for other uses) and rinse the rest under cold water.

Place the chicken and giblets in a large stockpot containing enough cold water to cover the bird. Add the salt and bring the pot slowly to a boil over medium-high heat, spooning off all of the scum that rises to the surface. When the scum no longer rises, reduce the heat to low or just so that the liquid barely simmers.

Add the onion, leeks, carrots, garlic, bay leaves, and peppercorns. Adjust the heat so that the liquid continues to simmer very gently (you should see only a very few bubbles) and cook for about 1 hour (more for a larger chicken), uncovered, turning the chicken over once, so that both sides poach uniformly. Test it for doneness by piercing one of its thighs with a fork. If the juices run clear, the chicken is done; if not, continue barely simmering it and checking it every 10 to 15 minutes. Once the chicken is done, remove it from the stock and allow it to cool slightly before deboning and shredding or dicing it, about 30 minutes.

Strain the stock into a large bowl and discard the vegetables and aromatics. Cool the stock and divide it into containers.

1 (4½- to 5-pound/2- to 2.3-kg) chicken with giblets and neck (preferably)

1 tablespoon fine sea salt

1 small white or yellow onion, whole and unpeeled

2 large leeks, washed and trimmed of tough leaves

1 large or 2 medium carrots, unpeeled

1 large head of garlic, unpeeled

2 bay leaves

12 peppercorns

NOTES: Empanada recipes usually call for a smaller amount of chicken. Therefore, if you can't use the remaining chicken, cool it and cover it with broth.

If refrigerated, the chicken will last, covered, for up to 2 days. Degrease the stock after it has chilled (a layer of fat will solidify on top, making it a cinch to remove). Freeze it in containers for up to 3 months. To thaw it, leave it in the refrigerator overnight; transfer it to a pot and heat it through at a low simmer.

★ CHAPTER 1 ★

EMPANADA DOUGH

THE FIRST EMPANADAS TO REACH THE NEW WORLD WERE MADE WITH WHEAT. LATIN AMERICANS, HOWEVER, USE MANY OTHER INGREDIENTS TO BUILD CASINGS FOR EMPANADAS.

In this chapter, you'll find a good compendium that includes the most popular kinds of dough used for empanadas from Mexico and Central America to the Latin Caribbean (including Cuba and the Dominican Republic), and all the way down to Argentina. Some dough fries crispy, other dough should be baked until it's flaky, and yet others produce a consistency similar to that of bread. You'll find dough made with root vegetables, nixtamalized corn, and plantains. You will find naturally gluten-free dough, such as one made with masa harina and another made with the precooked cornmeal of Venezuela (among others). Some, like the plantain and the cassava doughs, are both gluten free and ideal for a vegan diet. Of course, I've included the classic, wheat-flour pastry recipes too. And each recipe is clearly labeled as gluten free and/or vegan where relevant.

Each recipe in this chapter lists only the instructions for how to make the dough. You'll have to follow the instructions in each individual empanada recipe later on in the book for cutting, shaping, and cooking the empanadas, given that even two empanadas using the same dough may be made in completely different ways. For example, some of the empanadas using the Flaky Dough will be cut into small rounds and simply folded in half, while others may need larger rounds that can be placed atop each other to form ravioli-like empanadas.

MIXING AND MATCHING

In the empanada recipes that follow, I call for a specific kind of dough to be used in order to retain each recipe's authenticity. However, you should feel free to mix the fillings with the dough of your choice. For instance, if you prefer gluten-free dough to wheat dough, or vegan dough made with vegetable shortening instead of lard or butter, substitute it. The only caveat is that each recipe for dough makes a different amount. Also, some doughs will stretch, allowing more filling to be stuffed into the empanadas, while others won't. What this means is that if you substitute one for another, you may end up with extra filling. The easiest way to correct this is to make an extra batch (or two) of the gluten-free dough.

Not all dough is created equal, and while some types are ideal for baking, some must be fried or grilled. Each recipe is labeled with the required method of preparation so that you can tell them apart. Note that the wheat dough that I use for frying (Master Dough, page 29) may also be used for baked empanadas, so this is a great recipe that works for both

methods. Finally, all of the recipes in this book work with prepackaged frozen empanada discs.

MY NEW AND IMPROVED METHOD

What I bring to the table is a new method of working with dough that makes shaping empanada discs easy. Although most Latin American cooks use rolling pins to shape perfect dough rounds, I prefer to use a tortilla press for most of these recipes. Both methods work, of course, and I offer you both techniques, but using a tortilla press makes the process quicker and simpler (see below for a photo of the press in action).

ROLLING OUT DOUGH FOR EMPANADAS

Whether using a tortilla press or a rolling pin, below are some tips that should help you roll out dough more efficiently:

★ Before you roll any dough, it's important to let it rest for at least 10 minutes (or as long as the recipe calls for). This will allow you to roll the dough out without much shrinkage or resistance, helping it to keep its shape.

★ If a recipe calls for rolling out the dough onto a lightly floured surface, the bottom of the dough will most likely have remnants of that flour. This will prevent the scraps of dough from coming together so that they can be rolled again. Therefore, before you re-roll scraps of dough together, use a pastry brush to dust the flour off the bottom of the scraps.

★ Chilling butter-based dough will make it easier to roll out.

★ The less you have to roll out scraps of dough, the better. The dough will toughen if overworked. So, try to roll it out thinly and cut as many discs as you can from that first roll. Always cover the dough scraps and let them rest for at least 10 minutes before re-rolling.

★ Whether using a rolling pin or a tortilla press, use a zip-top freezer bag, open on three sides like a book, and place the empanada dough—usually shaped into balls or patties—in the middle of the open bag. Close the bag and shape the empanadas as directed in the recipe.

SWEET PLANTAIN DOUGH (PAGE 35) ON TORTILLA PRESS

MASTER DOUGH [PAGE 29]

SALTEÑA DOUGH [PAGE 32]

BREAD DOUGH [PAGE 30]

FLAKY DOUGH [PAGE 34]

MASA DOUGH

★ FRIED OR GRILLED ★ GLUTEN-FREE/VEGAN ★ MEXICO, GUATEMALA ★

3 cups (340 g) masa harina, plus more as needed

1 teaspoon fine sea salt

2 to 2½ cups (480 to 600 ml) warm water (110°F/43°C), plus more as needed

NOTE: The dough is best made just before using but, if needed, it can be made up to 4 hours ahead of time (keep it wrapped in plastic and refrigerated). Empanadas made with this masa dough can be filled up to 1 hour before cooking; keep them covered and refrigerated until ready to grill or fry (depending on what each recipe calls for). Once cooked, the empanadas freeze beautifully (see individual recipes for instructions).

In Mexico and Central America, you'll find empanadas made from corn that has been soaked in water mixed with lye (the chemical known in Spanish as *cal*). The process is called *nixtamalization* and it loosens the outer germ of the kernels, causing them to swell and become plump. The moist corn is then ground into masa or dried and ground into very fine flour called *masa harina*, used to make tortillas, empanadas, and other things. Empanadas made with this kind of dough can be either grilled or fried, depending on whether one wishes the dough to remain meaty in texture or to turn crispy. When working with masa harina, understand that brands will vary in the amount of water they'll need to reach the desired consistency. So I recommend testing the dough before rolling it, as described below, and always keeping the dough covered as you work, so it doesn't dry out. See opposite for more tips on working with this dough.

MAKES 12 EMPANADAS

In a large bowl, whisk together the masa harina and salt. Gradually add 2 cups (480 ml) of the warm water, kneading the mixture with your hand until it comes together into a ball with the consistency of mashed potatoes (if the dough is too dry, add a few more tablespoons of water at a time; if it's too wet, add a few tablespoons of the masa harina at a time). Turn the dough onto a clean surface and knead it until smooth, about 30 seconds or to the consistency of play dough; return it to the bowl, cover it with a damp kitchen towel, and let it rest for 10 minutes so that all of the liquid can be fully absorbed. To determine whether the dough is the proper consistency, shape a bit of the masa into a ball and press it flat into a disc. If the edges of the masa crack when shaped into discs, add a bit more water (a few tablespoons at a time); if the dough is too soft, add a bit more masa harina (a few tablespoons at a time).

See pages 49, 78, 101, 110, 122, and 136 for instructions on how to fill and shape the dough and recipes for empanadas that use this dough.

WORKING WITH MASA HARINA AND MASAREPA

Dough made with masa harina or masarepa can be finicky (see opposite and pages 26–27). They dry out very quickly if left uncovered or if the atmosphere is too dry. For this reason, always keep your dough covered as you work and follow the other tips below:

★ Keep a bowl of warm water next to you as you work so you can moisten the dough and rehydrate it as needed.

★ When pressing down the dough to shape rounds for the empanadas, the dough may crack along the edges—that means it is too dry. If that happens, moisten your hands with the warm water and press the dough back

into a ball with your moistened hands. That should add enough liquid for the dough not to crack anymore.

★ Before you shape the empanadas, always line a baking sheet with parchment paper to prevent them from sticking as they wait to be cooked. Also keep them covered with a lightly damp and clean kitchen towel (every bit of moisture helps).

★ You can shape empanadas made with either kind of masa up to 1 hour ahead of frying. In this case, cover them with a sheet of plastic wrap over the towel and refrigerate them until ready to cook.

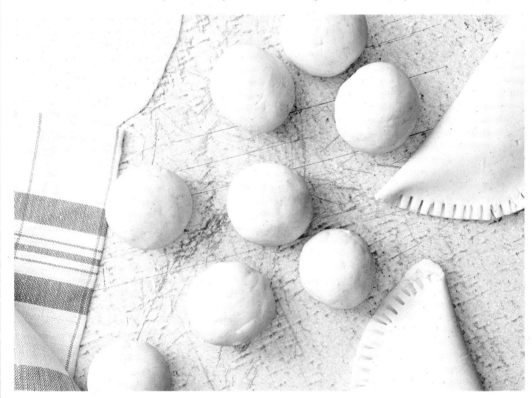

CORNMEAL DOUGH

+++

★ FRIED ★ GLUTEN-FREE/VEGAN ★ COLOMBIA, VENEZUELA ★

3 cups plus 2 tablespoons (440 g) precooked yellow cornmeal (*masarepa* or *harina pan*), plus more as needed

1 teaspoon fine sea salt

3 cups (720 ml) hot water (about 115°F/46°C), plus more as needed

In Colombia and Venezuela, you'll find empanadas made with golden, milled corn dough. Precooked cornmeal, known as *harina pan* or *masarepa*, is preferred to fresh-milled corn by most cooks because it only needs to be combined with warm liquid to become dough. It's found in stores that sell Latin American food products or online (see Sources, page 172). Note that regular cornmeal, such as the one used to make polenta, won't work here. See page 25 for tips on working with this dough.

+++

MAKES **15** TO **18** EMPANADAS

In a large bowl, whisk together the cornmeal and salt. Add the water slowly, in a thin stream, kneading the mixture with your hand until it comes together into a ball with the consistency of mashed potatoes (if the dough is too dry, add a few more tablespoons of water at a time; if it's too wet, add a few tablespoons of the precooked cornmeal at a time). Turn the dough onto a clean surface and knead it until smooth, 45 seconds to 1 minute or to the consistency of play dough. Return the dough to the bowl, cover it with plastic wrap or a damp kitchen towel, and let it rest for 10 minutes (to allow the fine grains to absorb all of the liquid).

See pages 52, 81, and 119 for instructions on how to fill and shape this dough and recipes for empanada fillings.

> **NOTE:** *Masarepa* is a product that has been made with precooked cornmeal (there is no need for you to cook it before using here). This dough is best made just before using and is not suitable for freezing. These empanadas can be shaped or filled up to 1 hour before frying as long as you keep them covered and chilled until you are ready to fry. Once fried, they freeze beautifully (see individual recipes for instructions).

CORNMEAL AND CASSAVA DOUGH

★ FRIED ★ GLUTEN-FREE/VEGAN ★ SOUTH AMERICA ★

In Colombia, empanadas from the Cauca region will sometimes be made with a mixture of precooked cornmeal (called *harina pan* or *masarepa)* and yuca or cassava flour called *almidón de yuca*, also known as tapioca starch or tapioca flour. Cassava flour produces both a crunchier crust (almost like a corn chip) and a chewier bite than dough made strictly with cornmeal. The dough is made golden with ground annatto seeds or with a product made of seasoned annatto, called Bijol, which is easy to find in Latin American supermarkets (see Sources, page 172). Use whichever is easier to find, as the taste will be the same. Try my tortilla press method (see page 22) to simplify the process or stay traditional and roll out the dough with a rolling pin. This is a terrific gluten-free recipe that can be used in place of the Master Dough (page 29) used for fried empanadas; they won't be authentic, but they will be delicious and wheat-free.

3 cups (420 g) precooked yellow cornmeal (*masarepa* or *harina pan*) (see Note), plus more as needed

½ cup (64 g) cassava flour or tapioca starch

1 teaspoon fine sea salt

1 teaspoon ground annatto (achiote) or Bijol

3 cups (720 ml) hot water (about 115°F/46°C), plus more as needed

MAKES 20 EMPANADAS

In a large bowl, whisk together the cornmeal, flour or starch, salt, and annatto or Bijol. Add the water slowly, in a thin stream, kneading the mixture with your hands until it comes together into a ball with the consistency of mashed potatoes (if the dough is too dry, add a few more tablespoons of water at a time; if it's too wet, add a few table-spoons of the precooked cornmeal at a time). Turn the dough onto a clean surface and knead it until smooth, 45 seconds to 1 minute or to the consistency of play dough. Return the dough to the bowl, cover it with plastic wrap or a damp kitchen towel, and let it rest for 10 minutes (to allow the fine grains to absorb all of the liquid).

See page 38 for instructions on how to fill and shape this dough and a recipe for an empanada that uses this dough.

> **NOTE:** *Masarepa* is a product that has been made with precooked cornmeal (there is no need for you to cook it before using here). Empanadas made with this dough must be fried as soon as they're shaped or they'll crack open. Plan to make the dough just before you have to fill the empanadas. This empanada dough is not suitable for freezing.

CASSAVA OR YUCA DOUGH

+++

★ FRIED ★ GLUTEN-FREE/VEGAN ★ LATIN CARIBBEAN, BRAZIL ★

1½ pounds (680 g) frozen, peeled cassava (yuca)

NOTE: This dough is best made just before frying. These empanadas must be fried as soon as they're shaped but freeze well after frying. When reheating, there is no need to thaw them; simply place them frozen into a hot oven (see individual recipes for additional instructions). If you wish to use this dough in place of a wheat-based dough in this book, plan to double this recipe so you have enough dough to use most of the filling. You can also create your own gluten-free recipes by filling empanadas made with this dough with any combination of ingredients, such as the Cooked Flank Steak (page 18) or Poached Chicken (page 19).

This hearty, gluten-free dough that tastes similar to potatoes creates golden empanadas with crispy exteriors that give way to chewy, meaty interiors. Cassava root is used abundantly throughout Latin America (where it's also known as yuca). It can be cooked, transformed into tapioca pearls, or ground into flour. In countries such as Brazil, the Dominican Republic, Cuba, Puerto Rico, and Panama, you'll find it used to make empanada dough. If you use it fresh, peel and section it before cooking it. I suggest you purchase frozen whole cassava, which you'll find in most supermarkets catering to Latinos, because it's already peeled and sectioned. Stay away from the canned stuff, as it is way too mushy and won't work. Whether fresh or frozen, yuca is easily boiled until fork tender. This dough is very sticky, so keep your hands moist every time you work with it. And because of the stickiness, it is particularly important to use my tortilla press method (see page 22), which makes shaping the discs much easier. Ideally you'll use a large food processor to make this dough. If you don't have one, use a potato masher to mash the yuca until smooth.

+++

MAKES **12** TO **14** EMPANADAS

Place the cassava in a large pot. Cover it with cold water and bring it to a boil over medium-high heat. Boil it for 15 to 20 minutes or until just fork tender (enough so that you can insert a fork into its flesh but still feel resistance in the center). Drain it and cool it slightly. Slice the pieces in half (lengthwise) and remove the tough fiber found in the middle; discard the fiber. Chop the cassava into smaller chunks and let it cool completely. Transfer the cassava to the bowl of a large food processor fitted with a metal blade, and pulse until it comes together into a ball, 25 to 35 one-second intervals. Turn the dough onto a sheet of plastic wrap and, using the wrap, shape it into a ball. Cover it with the plastic wrap and let it rest, at room temperature, for 30 minutes.

See pages 58 and 90 for instructions on how to fill and shape this dough and recipes for empanada fillings.

MASTER DOUGH

++

★ FRIED OR BAKED ★ VARIOUS COUNTRIES ★

When fried, this dough is flaky and crispy on the outside, yet tender on the inside. Its breadlike consistency holds the moistest fillings inside and pairs well with both sweet and savory flavors. This is my go-to dough whenever I want to make perfectly puffy empanadas. The acidity in the orange juice tenderizes the dough, although it doesn't add flavor. If you don't wish to fry empanadas made with this dough for health purposes, they can also be baked in a 400°F (205°C) oven until golden, for 8 to 12 minutes (15 to 20 minutes if frozen). They will bake into a softer consistency than when they're fried, and you won't be able to coat them in sugar (when called for), but they'll be just as delicious. Ideally you'll use a food processor to make this dough. If you don't have one, use a pastry cutter or two knives to cut the butter into the dry ingredients until it reaches the consistency of coarse sand; mix in the other ingredients by hand.

++

MAKES 36 TO 40 3-INCH (7.5-CM); 24 TO 26 3½-INCH (9-CM); OR 22 TO 26 3¾-INCH (9.5-CM) ROUNDS

Place the flour, baking powder, and salt in the bowl of a food processor fitted with a metal blade; pulse for 5 seconds to combine. Add the butter and pulse at 1-second intervals until the mixture resembles coarse sand, 20 to 25 pulses. Add the orange juice through the feed tube while pulsing at 1-second intervals, then add the seltzer water while pulsing, until the dough starts to come together into a ball, 30 to 35 pulses. Turn the dough onto a lightly floured surface and knead it for 1 to 2 minutes (the dough will look slightly cracked but it will smooth out when rolled out). Wrap the dough in plastic wrap and let it rest for 1 hour at room temperature.

See pages 61, 93, 96, and 113 for instructions on how to fill and shape this dough and recipes for empanada fillings.

3 cups (385 g) all-purpose flour, plus more for dusting

1 tablespoon baking powder

¼ teaspoon fine sea salt

½ cup (115 g) unsalted butter, cubed and chilled (or vegetable shortening)

1 tablespoon orange juice

⅔ cup (165 ml) seltzer water

NOTE: A tortilla press will not work well with this dough, as it must stretch out, which can only be done with a rolling pin. The rounds can be kept in the refrigerator, if well covered with plastic, for up to 48 hours before filling the empanadas. Let the chilled empanada rounds sit at room temperature for 10 minutes before filling. They can also be frozen (separated by parchment paper and stacked) in a plastic bin for up to 1 month. To thaw, let them sit at room temperature for 1 hour or until pliable. Once shaped, the empanadas can be frozen raw (see individual recipes for instructions).

BREAD DOUGH

+++

★ BAKED ★ VARIOUS COUNTRIES ★

8½ cups (1.1 kg) all-purpose flour, plus more for dusting

2 teaspoons fine sea salt

¾ cup (180 ml) melted pork or beef lard (or vegetable shortening)

2½ cups (600 ml) hot water (140°F/60°C)

Parchment paper cut into 28 (5-by-5-inch/12-by-12-cm) squares

NOTE: Some empanadas made with this dough will require them to be brushed with egg wash, while others will not. Adding egg wash will give a beautiful sheen to the finished empanadas. To make an egg wash, you can usually just whisk together 1 egg and 2 teaspoons water, although occasionally slightly different proportions are called for in the recipes, and sometimes milk replaces the water. This dough is best used right after making; once baked, the empanadas freeze beautifully (see individual recipes for instructions).

This is the classic recipe for dough that produces breadlike empanadas with crispy edges and paper-thin centers. The dough is extremely elastic and gives a lot when filled, allowing copious amounts of scrumptious ingredients to be stuffed inside. You'll want to start this dough long after the fillings are prepared and chilled, so that the empanadas can be filled shortly after the dough is made. This delicate dough must be cut while still warm. It's important to add the right amount of water—too little, and the dough will be brittle, but too much and the discs will stick to each other, making them a nightmare to shape. Keep extra flour nearby, and dust each disc after shaping it with a bit of flour so they won't stick together. I also stack the finished discs between pieces of waxed or parchment paper to prevent them from sticking together. If you're an advanced empanada maker, you may prefer to fill each empanada after shaping each disc. Many South American bakers prefer beef lard or suet (*grasa de pella*) to pork lard, but it's easier to find the latter; use either one in this recipe.

++

MAKES **22** TO **29** EMPANADAS

In a large bowl, whisk together the flour and salt. Make a well in the center. Add the lard and 2 cups (480 ml) of the water. Stir well with a spatula, until the dough starts coming together. Switch to your hands and add the remaining ½ cup (120 ml) water, kneading until the dough comes together (it will be soft and sticky). Turn the dough onto a well-floured surface and knead it for 1 to 2 minutes (adding more flour as needed), until the dough holds together in a ball and no longer sticks to your fingers. Return the dough to the bowl; cover it tightly with plastic wrap and let it rest for 10 minutes.

See pages 41, 66, 69, 84, 116, and 139 for instructions on how to fill and shape this dough and recipes for empanada fillings.

THE *REPULGUE* METHOD

Empanadas are sealed with a variety of methods. Sometimes the edges of the dough are simply pressed together, and sometimes the tines of a fork add decoration, while rustic folds are added to others. The most intricate design is created by the pinch-and-fold method used to seal South American empanadas, which creates ropelike edges. The method is called *repulgue,* because the thumb (*pulgar*) does most of the work.

To make the rope edges, you must form a rim (depending on the kind of dough you're using, you'll do this by either stretching it or by pressing it together), until it's about ½ inch (12 mm) wide.

Starting at one end of the empanada and using your right thumb and index finger, lift the dough and roll a small section of dough inward, pressing it into the rim (the index finger will be more like a guide). Repeat by grabbing another small section of dough right next to where

you pinched and, using your thumb and index fingers, roll it inward between your fingers and pinch it again into the rim, tightly. Keep doing this all around the edge and soon you'll see a ropelike design taking shape as you go.

Argentinean cooks say that a true empanada has thirteen *repulgues.* The smaller the sections you pinch, the more detailed the rope design will be. If your edges look more like crimped pie dough than ropes, don't worry. That means that you're leaving too much space between the sections you're rolling. Instead, I suggest that you let them overlap slightly onto each other as you roll. Once you get the hang of it, you'll be rolling and pinching in no time. For practice, use a napkin until you feel comfortable working with the dough.

This method works best with the Bread Dough (opposite) and with store-bought *hojaldrada* empanada discs. It also works with the *Salteña* Dough (page 32) and with the Master Dough (page 29).

SALTEÑA DOUGH

1 cup (240 ml) melted lard (or vegetable shortening)

1 tablespoon whole annatto (achiote) seeds (see Sources, page 172)

9½ cups (1.2 kg) all-purpose flour, plus more for dusting

½ cup (100 g) sugar

1 teaspoon fine sea salt

2 large egg yolks

3 cups (720ml) hot water (115°F/46°C), plus more as needed

NOTE: This dough cannot be frozen and is best used after resting for 1 hour; once baked, the empanadas freeze beautifully (see individual recipes for instructions).

Bolivia is famous for the football-shaped *salteñas* made with slightly sweetened, annatto-tinted dough. They encase savory stews made with beef, chicken, or both (called *jigote*). The fillings, which always include potatoes and peas, are so moist that they must first be thickened with gelatin so that they can be stuffed into the dough. Once baked, the gelatin melts and the fillings become soupy. *Salteñas* have flat bottoms that help them stand on their own. Their edges bake to a deep caramel (sometimes black) color, while the rest of the dough develops a golden hue. The proper way to eat a *salteña* is to bite off one of the ends and to drink any juices before cutting into the filling. Note that the dough must rest for a long time before you can roll it out. This time allows the gluten in the flour to relax, and makes it easier to roll the dough without too much shrinkage.

MAKES 26 TO 28 *SALTEÑAS*

In a medium saucepan set over medium heat, combine the lard and annatto seeds and heat until they begin to bubble slightly, about 2 minutes. Immediately remove the pot from the heat and steep the seeds for 15 minutes. Strain the lard into a medium bowl; discard the seeds. Cool the lard completely.

In a large bowl, whisk together the flour, sugar, and salt. Make a well in the center and add the egg yolks and cooled lard. Using a wooden spatula, begin to mix everything together while slowly adding enough of the hot water that the dough holds together (it will be wet and sticky). Turn the dough onto a well-floured surface and knead it for 2 to 3 minutes (adding more flour as needed), until the dough is smooth, comes together into a ball, and springs back when gently pressed with a fingertip. Return it to the bowl; cover the dough tightly with plastic wrap and let it rest for 45 to 60 minutes.

See pages 72 and 125 for instructions on how to fill and shape this dough and recipes for empanada fillings.

PASTÉIS DOUGH

★ FRIED ★ BRAZIL ★

Brazilian fried empanadas made with this lard-based dough are called *pastéis* (pronounced *pahs-teys*). The dough is supple and fries up blistery, crispy, and with a light and flaky texture, very much like that of egg roll dough. The dough itself can be made easily in a bowl, but you'll need a little bit of time and patience to roll out the dough and to cut it into squares. In order to get crackly, blistery dough when fried, it must first be rolled out very thinly. The dough needs to rest before you roll it, so that the gluten in the flour can relax and allow it to stretch thinly; otherwise your squares will shrink into small, fat rectangles. If at first you find it hard to roll out the dough thinly, don't worry; the *pastéis* will still be delicious. Once the dough is cut, you can layer it between sheets of parchment paper on a baking sheet and let it rest for 20 minutes (or refrigerate it for up to 2 hours) before filling and frying the *pastéis*. Always place the filling on the sticky side of the pastry (one side will be drier than the other) so that the edges will stick together and seal tightly. In a pinch, you can substitute this dough with egg roll wrappers, but you'll need to moisten their edges with egg wash in order to make them stick.

MAKES 12 *PASTÉIS*

In a large bowl, whisk together the flour and salt. Make a well in the center. Add the lard or shortening and vinegar. Begin to mix the wet ingredients into the flour with a spoon as you add the water in a stream. When all the water has been added, switch to your hands and knead the dough until it comes together into a ball. Turn out the dough onto a lightly floured surface and knead until it is smooth, about 1 minute. Roll it out into a rectangle about 2 inches (5 cm) thick (this will make it easier to roll out fully) and wrap it in plastic; let it rest for 20 minutes.

See pages 55, 87, 130, 151, and 154 for instructions on how to fill and shape this dough and recipes for empanada fillings.

2½ cups (315 g) all-purpose flour, plus more for dusting

1 teaspoon fine sea salt

⅓ cup (75 ml) melted lard (or vegetable shortening)

1 tablespoon white vinegar

⅔ cup (165 ml) warm water (100°F/38°C)

NOTE: This dough cannot be frozen and is best used after resting for 20 minutes; once shaped, the empanadas can be frozen raw (see individual recipes for instructions).

FLAKY DOUGH

★ BAKED ★ VARIOUS COUNTRIES ★

1½ cups (170 g) all-purpose flour, plus more for dusting

2 tablespoons sugar

Pinch of fine sea salt

8 ounces (225 g) cream cheese, cubed and chilled

½ cup (115 g) unsalted butter, cubed and chilled

NOTE: The dough will keep in your refrigerator for up to 2 days—any longer and it will fall apart. You can freeze the dough up to 2 months and thaw the dough in the refrigerator overnight, before proceeding with shaping the empanadas. You can also cut the dough into discs, stack them (with parchment paper in between), and freeze them for up to 2 months; thaw them in the refrigerator overnight before proceeding with filling and baking the empanadas. You can assemble the empanadas up to 8 hours before baking, or freeze them unbaked (see instructions in individual recipes).

In Latin America, this dough is also known as *masa hojaldrada*. Technically, it's only made with butter, but growing up in Guatemala, I learned that hot weather and cold butter don't always play together nicely. Cream cheese, on the other hand, stands up to the heat, stays solid longer, and contains enough acidity to produce a tender pastry. As the cheese melts, it creates steam that results in deliciously flaky pastry. Empanadas made with this dough should be brushed with egg wash (for sheen) and should be refrigerated for at least 10 minutes (and up to overnight) before they're baked so that they'll keep their shape; these two steps will also prevent the dough from getting soggy. Ideally you'll use a food processor to make this dough. If you don't have one, use a pastry cutter or two knives to cut the butter and cream cheese into the dough until it reaches the consistency of coarse sand; then mix by hand.

MAKES ABOUT 22 (4-INCH/10-CM); 32 (3½-INCH/9-CM); 36 (3¼-INCH/8-CM); 40 (3-INCH/7.5-CM); OR 48 (2½-INCH/6-CM) DISCS

In the bowl of a food processor fitted with a metal blade, combine the flour, sugar, and salt; pulse for 20 seconds, or until combined. Add the cream cheese and butter and pulse until the mixture comes together and forms a ball, about 2 minutes (about 125 one-second pulses). Remove the pastry from the food processor, and divide it in half. Shape each half into a flat disc; wrap each disc in plastic wrap, and chill them for at least 30 minutes or up to 48 hours.

See pages 44, 46, 98, 106, 144, 148, and 157 for instructions on how to fill and shape this dough and recipes for empanada fillings.

SWEET PLANTAIN DOUGH

★ FRIED ★ GLUTEN-FREE/VEGAN ★ VARIOUS COUNTRIES ★

This dough is made with plantains that have been allowed to ripen until their skins are golden. As the plantains boil, their skins shrink and the flesh expands. As soon as the skins begin to split open, they are ready to transform into dough. Look for large plantains that are wider, rather than longer, about 2 inches (5 cm) in diameter. Thinner plantains take much longer to ripen and sometimes never soften quite enough to use for this. I prefer to purchase a couple of extra plantains in case they ripen at different rates. When they're still green, I place them in paper bags and allow them to ripen for a couple of days.

MAKES 12 TO 14 EMPANADAS

With a sharp knife, cut off the tips of the plantains, then slice the plantains in half crosswise. Place them in a large pot; cover with water and add the salt. Bring the pot to a boil over high heat. Boil the plantains until they're fork tender and their skins split, 20 to 22 minutes. Transfer the plantains to a large bowl; drain them well and allow them to cool completely, about 15 minutes. Peel the plantains and mash them well with a fork or a potato masher, until smooth. If the dough is too loose, you can add flour (see Notes). Use immediately.

See page 75 for instructions on how to fill and shape this dough and a recipe for an empanada filling.

4 large yellow plantains (about 2½ pounds/1.2 kg)

1 tablespoon fine sea salt

⅓ cup (40 g) all-purpose flour (or rice or chickpea flour for gluten-free), if needed (see Notes)

> **NOTES:** Chances are that if the dough is not holding together, your plantains were too ripe. Take a bit of dough in your hands and press it together; if it holds together well, it's ready. If the plantains are too loose, add some flour (1 tablespoon at a time) and stir it into the dough until it holds together (use gluten-free flour to keep them gluten-free).
>
> This dough must be used directly after making it and is not suitable for freezing. Once the empanadas are cooked, they can be frozen (see instructions in individual recipes).

CHAPTER 2

★ ★

+++

VEGETABLE,

NUT ◆◆◆ & ◆◆◆ CHEESE EMPANADAS

MOM WAS RIGHT WHEN SHE SAID YOU SHOULD EAT YOUR VEGETABLES. HOWEVER, VEGETABLES DON'T HAVE TO BE BORING, AND THIS CHAPTER PROVES JUST THAT.

Here, you'll find vegetarian corn empanadas from Argentina, so sweet and spicy that you'll have trouble eating only one. You'll also discover bean empanadas made with authentic corn crusts. You will come across the spinach and cheese empanadas from Argentina that feature classic Italian flavors. You'll discover the flaky Brazilian pies made with hearts of palm, and the Ecuadorian onion pies that are sweet enough to serve as part of a dessert course. The empanadas made with cassava crust and simply stuffed with cheese will make you wonder how such complex flavor can result from only a couple of ingredients. And the Colombian empanadas stuffed with peanuts and potatoes will surprise with their elegant and subtle taste. Some of the hand-held pies can be part of an appetizer platter, while others can become the main component of a meal. Not all vegetable empanadas in Latin America (or in this chapter) are vegetarian because some dough is made with lard, but this is an easy thing to change simply by switching to vegetable shortening. However, all of these empanadas are perfectly delectable and will have you begging for second servings of vegetables every time.

SPICY POTATO AND PEANUT EMPANADAS

★ EMPANADAS DE PIPIÁN ★ COLOMBIA ★

2 tablespoons extra-virgin olive oil

1 cup (120 g) finely chopped white onions

½ cup (50 g) finely chopped leeks (white and light green parts only)

3 large cloves garlic, minced

1 teaspoon ground annatto (achiote) or Bijol (see Notes)

1 cup (185 g) seeded and finely chopped plum tomatoes

½ cup (60 g) roasted red bell pepper (see page 15), cored, seeded, and finely chopped

1 small serrano pepper, finely chopped (with seeds)

2 teaspoons fine sea salt

2 teaspoons ground cumin

1 cup (150 g) ground roasted peanuts (unsalted or lightly salted preferred)

3 cups (455 g) peeled and finely diced Yukon gold potatoes, boiled until fork tender

1 recipe Cornmeal and Cassava Dough (page 27)

Vegetable oil for frying

These gluten-free and vegetarian empanadas are spicy, comforting, and exotic all at the same time. They combine the best of African and native Colombian flavors that define the cuisine of the Cauca region. The tomato-based sauce that moistens the filling is called *hogao*, and although most times it's not spicy, my recipe carries a good kick courtesy of a hot chile. The potatoes must be diced finely and then cooked just until tender, so that each cube can retain its shape. The result is perhaps the most elegant empanada you'll find in the Latin American culinary landscape, juxtaposing creamy and crunchy textures that explode on the palate. In Bogota, they're served as tiny appetizers, dipped into a silken peanut sauce (see Creamy Peanut Sauce, page 165). My empanadas are on the larger side and I serve them as an entree.

+++

MAKES 20 EMPANADAS

MAKE THE FILLING: Heat the olive oil in a large skillet over medium-high heat. Add the onions, leeks, garlic, and annatto or Bijol and sauté them for 1 minute, or until fragrant. Add the tomatoes, bell pepper, serrano pepper, salt, and cumin; continue cooking until the mixture has thickened, about 3 minutes. Remove it from the heat and add the peanuts and potatoes. Cover and chill the filling for at least 4 hours or overnight.

ASSEMBLE THE EMPANADAS: After the filling chills, make the dough as directed on page 27. Line two large baking sheets with parchment paper; set them aside. Divide the dough into 20 equal pieces (about 2½ ounces/70 g each). Roll each portion into a ball and keep them covered with a damp kitchen

Continued →

towel as you work. Line a tortilla press with a zip-top freezer bag that has been cut open on three sides so that it opens like a book. Place a ball of dough in the middle of the tortilla press and flatten it into a 5½-inch (14-cm) round, about ⅛ inch (3 mm) thick (or roll it out with a rolling pin). Place 3 heaping tablespoons of the filling in the middle of the round, leaving a small rim. Use the bag to fold the dough over the filling, forming a half-moon; press the edges together with your fingers to seal. Transfer the empanada to a prepared baking sheet. Repeat with the rest of the dough and filling, keeping the empanadas covered as you go.

FRY THE EMPANADAS AND SERVE: Fit a large pan with a metal cooling rack and set it aside. In a large skillet with high sides, heat 1 to 1½ inches (2.5 to 3 cm) of vegetable oil to 360°F (180°C). You may also use a deep-fryer according to the manufacturer's directions. Working in batches of 4 or 5 empanadas at a time, carefully slide them into the oil and fry them until golden, 3 to 4 minutes, turning them over halfway through. If the oil gets too hot as you fry and they're browning too quickly, lower the temperature and let the oil cool slightly before frying any more. Use a slotted spoon to transfer the fried empanadas to the prepared rack to drain. Serve them immediately or keep them warm in a 250°F (120°C) oven for up to 1 hour before serving.

NOTES: Once fried, these can be frozen for up to 3 months. Freeze them in a single layer on baking sheets lined with parchment paper; once frozen solid, these can be transferred to freezer boxes or zip-top bags. Reheat them at 350°F (175°C) for 12 to 15 minutes or until their centers are hot.

Bijol is a seasoning made with powdered annatto, which dissolves quickly in liquid and tints food yellow. If you use annatto paste in its place, dissolve it in an equal amount of hot water or stock before using it. See Sources (page 172).

CHEESY SPINACH EMPANADAS

These plump hand-held pies embellished by ropelike edges are stuffed with a hearty, creamy, and comforting filling. I first ate these empanadas in the Argentinean Embassy in Guatemala back in the 1970s. Years later, riding the subway in Toronto, Canada, I overheard two Argentinean cooks comparing notes on their spinach empanadas. I paid close attention. One lady claimed that adding a lot of onions kept the filling moist, while the other insisted that her secret was to add an abundant amount of cheese. This recipe combines the best of what they each had to offer. My big regret is never having had the chance to thank them for the free cooking lesson.

MAKES 28 EMPANADAS

MAKE THE FILLING: Heat the oil in a large skillet with high sides over medium-high heat. Add the onions and cook, stirring, until softened, about 3 minutes. Add the garlic and cook for 20 seconds. Add the spinach in batches, stirring it in well (it will cook down to fit in the skillet). Cook until there is no liquid left and the spinach is cooked through, 8 to 10 minutes (the spinach will still be moist). Stir in the salt, pepper, and nutmeg. Remove the filling to a bowl and let it cool completely; cover and chill it for 2 hours. Stir in the mozzarella, ricotta, and Parmesan to combine; chill the filling again, covered, until ready to use.

ASSEMBLE THE EMPANADAS: After the filling chills, make the dough as directed on page 30 and let it rest, covered with plastic wrap, for 10 minutes at room temperature. Divide the dough into 28 equal pieces (about 2 ounces/55 g each). Roll each piece into a ball, folding the bottom of the dough onto itself so that the ends are at the bottom and the tops are smooth (the way

Continued ➡

2 tablespoons extra-virgin olive oil

1 cup (120 g) finely chopped white onions

2 large cloves garlic, minced

1 pound (455 g) washed, drained, and chopped fresh spinach or baby spinach

1 teaspoon fine sea salt

¼ teaspoon freshly ground black pepper

¼ teaspoon freshly grated nutmeg

2½ cups (300 g) shredded mozzarella

1¾ cups (420 ml) whole milk ricotta

½ cup (60 g) grated Parmesan cheese

1 recipe Bread Dough (page 30)

Egg wash, made with 1 beaten egg and 2 teaspoons water

you'd shape rolls). Place them on a lightly floured baking sheet and cover them with a clean towel; let them rest for 10 minutes. On a well-floured surface, press each ball slightly into a disc. Line a tortilla press with a zip-top freezer bag that has been cut open on three sides so that it opens like a book. Place a disc in the middle of the tortilla press and flatten it into a 5-inch (12-cm) round, about ⅛ inch (3 mm) thick (or roll it out with a rolling pin). Stack the discs with parchment paper in between to avoid sticking.

Line three baking sheets with parchment paper; set them aside. Place 2 heaping tablespoons of the filling in the center of each disc. Fold the bottom of the dough to meet the top of the disc, encasing the filling and forming a half-moon, and press the edges together well. Make ½-inch (12-mm) edges by pressing the rims between your fingers using the *repulgue* method (see page 31). The empanadas can sit at room temperature uncovered for 20 minutes before baking or can be refrigerated for up to 1 hour before baking.

BAKE THE EMPANADAS AND SERVE: Preheat the oven to 450°F (230°C). Place the empanadas on the prepared pans and brush them with the egg wash. Bake the empanadas for 28 to 30 minutes, or until golden (rotate the pans in the oven halfway through baking, back to front and top to bottom, to ensure that all of the empanadas bake evenly). Transfer the empanadas to a cooling rack; let them cool for 10 minutes before serving.

NOTE: To freeze these empanadas, cool them to room temperature; set them in a single layer on a baking sheet and freeze them until solid. When solid, transfer them to zip-top bags or freezer boxes and freeze them for up to 4 months. Reheat them in a 350°F (175°C) oven until warmed through, 10 to 15 minutes.

CORN AND SPANISH SMOKED PAPRIKA TURNOVERS

+++

★ EMPANADITAS DE CHOCLO ★ ARGENTINA ★

2 tablespoons unsalted butter

½ cup (60 g) finely chopped white onion

½ cup (50 g) finely chopped red bell pepper

1 large clove garlic, minced

2 teaspoons smoked Spanish paprika (pimentón)

1 teaspoon ground cumin

1 teaspoon fine sea salt

2 cups (330 g) corn kernels (fresh or frozen and thawed)

1 tablespoon all-purpose flour

¾ cup (180 ml) whole milk

1 recipe Flaky Dough (page 34)

Egg wash, made with 1 beaten egg and 2 teaspoons water

The filling for these dainty corn turnovers with pinched edges, also known as *empanaditas de humitas*, is a little bit spicy and very smoky thanks to the gutsy kick of smoked Spanish paprika. Argentinean cooks scrape corn off the cob, but frozen (and thawed) corn kernels work great too. Some cooks add green olives, green onions, cheese, or hard-boiled eggs, but I'm more of a purist and like the corn to take center stage, as it does in this rendition. You can make larger empanadas with store-bought empanada discs (you'll need sixteen). Using the Flaky Dough on page 34 is my favorite way because the small amount of sugar in the dough enhances the sweetness of the corn, elevating the empanadas to a sublime level of exquisiteness.

+++

MAKES 32 EMPANADAS

MAKE THE FILLING: In a large sauté pan with high sides, melt the butter over medium-high heat. Add the onion, pepper, and garlic; cook, stirring, until the onion has softened, about 4 minutes. Add the paprika, cumin, and salt; stir to combine. Add the corn and cook, stirring, for 2 minutes.

Add the flour and stir to combine; cook, stirring, for 1 minute. Add the milk all at once, and cook, stirring constantly, until the mixture has thickened, about 1 minute. Remove the filling from the heat and let it cool completely; transfer it to a small bowl, cover it with plastic wrap, and chill it for at least 30 minutes (preferably overnight).

ASSEMBLE THE EMPANADAS: After the filling chills, make the dough as directed on page 34 and let it rest, wrapped in plastic, in the refrigerator for at least 30 minutes or up to 24 hours (if the dough is too cold to roll, let it sit at room temperature for 10 minutes before rolling).

Line two large baking sheets with parchment paper; set them aside. On a well-floured surface and with a well-floured rolling pin, roll out the pastry to about ⅛ inch (3 mm) thick (like for piecrust). Keep lightly dusting flour on your surface and rolling pin as you roll so that the pastry doesn't tear or stick (see Notes). Using a 3½-inch (9-cm) round cutter, cut 32 rounds, rolling and cutting the scraps as needed. Keep them covered as you work. Place about 2 teaspoons of the filling on the bottom half of each pastry round; brush the edges with egg wash and fold them in half over the filling to form half-moons. Seal the edges of the empanadas very well with your fingers and make a ½-inch (3-mm) edge. Starting on one end of the edge, use your thumb and forefinger to make pointy crimps about five times along the edges. Transfer the empanadas to the baking sheets and chill them uncovered for 20 minutes (or up to 8 hours).

BAKE THE EMPANADAS AND SERVE: Preheat oven to 400°F (205°C). Brush the tops of the empanadas with the egg wash. Bake them for 12 to 15 minutes, until golden (rotate the pans in the oven halfway through baking, back to front and top to bottom, to ensure that all of the empanadas bake evenly). Let them rest for 3 minutes and serve them warm.

NOTES: This is sticky dough. For easier rolling, roll the pastry on a generously floured surface, flour the top of the pastry, and place a piece of plastic wrap (or parchment paper) directly over the top of the pastry so that the rolling pin doesn't stick. If you need to re-roll the dough, brush excess flour off the scraps with a clean pastry brush and gather up the scraps; wrap them in plastic and chill them for 10 minutes.

Assemble the empanadas ahead and chill them for up to 8 hours before baking. Or freeze them on the prepared sheet, unbaked; once solid, transfer them to freezer-safe containers and keep them frozen for up to 4 months. Bake them directly from the freezer, adding a few minutes to the baking time, or until they're golden.

ROQUEFORT AND WALNUT MINI PIES

+++

★ EMPANADITAS DE QUESO Y NUECES ★ ARGENTINA, CHILE ★

6 ounces (170 g) Roquefort cheese, crumbled

4 ounces (115 g) cream cheese, softened to room temperature

½ cup (55 g) chopped walnuts

1 recipe Flaky Dough (page 34)

Honey for drizzling

Egg wash, made with 1 beaten egg and 2 teaspoons water

These empanadas are pungent, sweet, and nutty all at the same time. They're among the most elegant of all of the hand-held pies you'll find in South America. I've had these in the homes of both Argentinean and Chilean friends, where they're usually served as part of canapé platters during cocktail hour or as a component of a cheese course. You'll love the fact that they can be made and frozen unbaked way ahead of time. Come time to cook them, you won't even have to thaw them, as they can go directly from freezer to oven. I like to offer these on large trays arranged with clusters of grapes on either end. Even if you think you don't like blue cheese, give these a try; the sweetness of the honey intermingled with the buttery pastry helps to mellow the bite of the blue veins in the cheese. I like these empanadas relatively small—just the right size that you can nibble on several of them, because after you try one, you will undoubtedly crave another.

+++

MAKES 32 EMPANADAS

MAKE THE FILLING: In a medium bowl, mix together the cheeses and the nuts. Turn the mixture over onto a large piece of plastic wrap; roll it into a log, and chill it for at least 30 minutes (or overnight).

ASSEMBLE THE EMPANADAS: While the filling chills, make the dough as directed on page 34 and let it rest, wrapped in plastic, in the refrigerator for at least 30 minutes or up to 24 hours (if the dough is too cold to roll, let it sit at room temperature for 10 minutes before rolling). Line two large baking sheets with parchment paper; set them aside.

Continued ➜

ROQUEFORT AND
WALNUT MINI PIES

CORN AND SPANISH SMOKED
PAPRIKA TURNOVERS (PAGE 44)

On a well-floured surface and with a well-floured rolling pin, roll out the pastry to about ⅛ inch (3 mm) thick (like for piecrust). Keep lightly dusting flour on your surface and rolling pin as you roll so that the pastry doesn't tear or stick (see Notes). Using a 3½-inch (9-cm) round cutter, cut 32 rounds, rolling and cutting the scraps as needed. Keep them covered as you work.

Place 2 teaspoons of the cheese filling on the bottom half of each pastry round and drizzle it lightly with about ¼ teaspoon honey; brush the edges of the rounds with the egg wash and fold them in half over the filling to form half-moons. Seal the edges of the empanadas very well with your fingers and crimp them shut tight with the tines of a fork. It's important to seal these empanadas very well, or you'll have cheese leakage. Use the tines of the fork to poke vents on top of each empanada. Transfer the empanadas to the baking sheets and chill them uncovered for 20 minutes (or up to 8 hours).

BAKE THE EMPANADAS AND SERVE: Preheat the oven to 400°F (205°C). Brush the tops of the empanadas with the egg wash. Bake until they are golden, 12 to 14 minutes (rotate the pans in the oven halfway through baking, back to front and top to bottom, to ensure that all of the empanadas bake evenly). Let them rest for 2 to 3 minutes and serve them warm.

NOTES: This is sticky dough. For easier rolling, roll the pastry on a generously floured surface, flour the top of the pastry, and use a piece of plastic wrap (or parchment paper) directly over the top of the pastry so that the rolling pin doesn't stick. If you need to re-roll the dough, brush excess flour off the scraps with a clean pastry brush and gather up the scraps; wrap them in plastic and chill them for 10 minutes.

To freeze the unbaked empanadas, do not brush the tops with egg wash. Place them in one layer on the prepared baking sheets and freeze them until solid. Transfer them to freezer-safe containers and keep them frozen for up to 4 months. To bake, brush the tops of the frozen empanadas with the egg wash. Bake them directly from the freezer, adding 3 to 5 more minutes to the baking time, until they are golden.

CHEESE AND LOROCO MASA PIES

++

★ DOBLADAS DE LOROCO ★ GUATEMALA ★

I ate *dobladas* such as these several times in the city of Antigua, Guatemala, where they drenched them in rich tomato sauce. Their name indicates that the dough has been folded in half (*doblar*) to resemble a half-moon shape. If you were to eat these in Mexico, they'd simply be known as *quesadillas de loroco,* but in Central American territory, their name changes. Crispy masa dough surrounds these vegetarian empanadas made with the buds of a wildflower that grows in Central America, called *loroco*. Loroco can be found frozen or in jars and its taste is reminiscent of asparagus and artichokes (which you can substitute in a pinch). If you like the idea of serving them with a red sauce, try the Dried Chile, Bell Pepper, and Tomato Sauce on page 169, but if you prefer a lighter one, serve it with the Raw Tomatillo Salsa on page 171.

++

MAKES **12** *DOBLADAS*

MAKE THE FILLING: In a medium bowl, stir together the tomatoes, loroco, mozzarella, queso seco or feta, oregano, salt, and pepper until combined. Cover and chill the filling for at least 30 minutes, or overnight.

ASSEMBLE THE *DOBLADAS*: After the filling chills, make the dough as directed on page 24 and let it rest, covered with plastic or with a damp towel, for 10 minutes at room temperature.

Line a large baking sheet with parchment paper; set it aside. Divide the dough into 12 equal portions (about 2½ ounces/70 g each). Roll each portion into a ball and keep them covered with a damp kitchen towel as you work. Line a tortilla press with

1 cup (185 g) seeded and minced plum tomatoes (see Notes)

1 cup (115 g) chopped loroco buds (fresh, frozen and thawed, or drained from a jar)

½ cup (60 g) shredded whole milk mozzarella

½ cup (60 g) shredded queso seco or crumbled feta cheese

½ teaspoon crushed Mexican oregano

¼ teaspoon fine sea salt, or to taste

¼ teaspoon freshly ground black pepper, or to taste

1 recipe Masa Dough (page 24)

Vegetable oil for frying

1 recipe Raw Tomatillo Salsa (page 171) or Dried Chile, Bell Pepper, and Tomato Sauce (page 169)

1 cup (240 ml) Mexican crema or crème fraîche

Continued ➡

a zip-top freezer bag that has been cut open on three sides so that it opens like a book. Place a ball of masa in the middle of the tortilla press and flatten it into a 5½-inch (14-cm) disc about ⅛ inch (3 mm) thick. If you don't have a tortilla press, use a flat-bottomed, heavy skillet to press the dough. Place 2 heaping tablespoons of the loroco filling in the middle of the round, leaving a small rim. Use the bag to fold the masa over the filling, forming a half-moon. Press the edges together with your fingers to seal, and use a fork to crimp the edges. Transfer the *doblada* to the prepared baking sheet. Repeat with the rest of the dough and filling, keeping the *dobladas* covered as you go.

FRY THE *DOBLADAS* AND SERVE: Fit a large baking sheet with a metal cooling rack; set it aside. In a large skillet with high sides, heat 1 to 1½ inches (2.5 to 4 cm) of oil to 360°F (180°C) or use a deep-fryer according to the manufacturer's directions. Working in batches, carefully slide the *dobladas* into the oil. Fry them until golden, 4 to 6 minutes, turning them over halfway though. If the oil gets too hot as you fry and they're browning too quickly, lower the temperature and let the oil cool slightly before frying any more. Use a slotted spoon to transfer the fried *dobladas* to the prepared rack to drain. Serve them immediately with salsa and a dollop of crema or crème fraîche or keep the *dobladas* warm for up to 1 hour in a 250°F (120°C) oven.

NOTES: If your tomatoes are overly ripe, slice them in half and squeeze them in your hands in order to remove some of the juices (so that the filling isn't too watery), then dice.

To freeze the *dobladas*, place the fried *dobladas* in a single layer on a baking sheet lined with parchment paper; freeze them until solid and then transfer them to freezer-safe bags or bins. They keep frozen for up to 3 months. Reheat them in a 350°F (175°C) oven for 12 to 15 minutes, or until the filling is hot.

BLACK BEAN AND CHEESE "DOMINO" PIES

+++

★ EMPANADAS DOMINÓ ★ VENEZUELA ★

2 tablespoons extra-virgin olive oil

1 cup (120 g) minced white onions

½ cup (50 g) minced leek (white and light green parts only)

1 *aji dulce* (sweet Caribbean pepper) or serrano pepper, seeded and minced

1 large clove garlic, minced

1 teaspoon ground annatto (achiote) or Bijol (see Notes on page 40)

1½ teaspoons ground cumin

1 tablespoon tomato paste

1 tablespoon Worcestershire sauce

2 (15-ounce/430-g) cans whole black beans, drained and rinsed

1 teaspoon fine sea salt, or to taste

¼ teaspoon freshly ground black pepper

1 recipe Cornmeal Dough (page 26)

6 ounces (170 g) queso blanco or mozzarella cheese, shredded

Vegetable oil for frying

These corn empanadas are filled with a luscious, gooey, and toothsome black-and-white filling; hence, their name. Some cooks prefer to roll the dough into thick discs, which yield a meatier texture. I like mine rolled somewhat thin because they produce crispier empanadas. To do this, I use my unorthodox but efficient tortilla press method (see page 22). Normally, cooks will roll the dough inside plastic wrap, using a rolling pin, then cut the rounds with a plate or cup, instead of using a tortilla press—but either technique works, of course. These pies are quick to assemble and offer a protein-packed vegetarian option. Canned beans are great to have on hand for whenever you wish to make these. If you happen to have leftover shredded beef (see page 18) and some fried plantains, add a bit to the filling and you'll have empanadas based on Venezuela's national dish, called *pabellón*. I serve these with tomato and onion salad, lightly dressed with lemon vinaigrette.

+++

MAKES 18 EMPANADAS

MAKE THE FILLING: In a large skillet, heat the olive oil over medium-high heat. Add the onions, leeks, *aji* or serrano pepper, garlic, annatto or Bijol, and cumin. Cook until the onions have softened, 4 to 6 minutes. Add the tomato paste and Worcestershire sauce; stir well and cook for 30 seconds. Add 1 cup (240 ml) water, the beans, salt, and black pepper; bring them to a boil, lower the heat to medium, and simmer for 10 minutes or until they have thickened, stirring regularly. Remove the filling from the heat and let it cool; cover and chill it thoroughly (at least 1 hour or overnight).

Continued ➜

ASSEMBLE THE EMPANADAS: After the filling chills, make the dough as directed on page 26 and let it rest, covered with plastic or with a damp towel, for 10 minutes at room temperature.

Line a large baking sheet with parchment paper; set it aside. Divide the dough into 18 equal pieces (about 2 ounces/55 g each). Line a tortilla press with a zip-top freezer bag that has been cut open on three sides so that it opens like a book. Place a ball of dough in the middle of the tortilla press and flatten it into a 5-inch (12-cm) round, about ⅛ inch (3 mm) thick. If you don't have a tortilla press, flatten each ball using a flat-bottomed, heavy skillet.

Place 2 tablespoons of the filling and 1 tablespoon of the cheese in the middle of the round, leaving a small rim. Use the bag to fold the dough over the filling, forming a half-moon. Press the edges together with your fingers to seal. Transfer the empanada to the prepared baking sheet. Repeat with the rest of the dough and filling, keeping the empanadas covered as you go. These empanadas can be shaped and filled up to 1 hour before frying as long as you keep them covered and chilled until you're ready to fry.

FRY THE EMPANADAS AND SERVE: Fit a large baking sheet with a metal cooling rack and set it aside. In a large skillet with high sides, heat 1 to 1½ inches (2.5 to 4 cm) of vegetable oil to 360°F (180°C). You may also use a deep-fryer according to the manufacturer's directions. Working in batches of 4 or 5 empanadas at a time, carefully slide them into the oil. Fry them until golden, 3 to 4 minutes, turning them over halfway through. If the oil gets too hot as you fry and they're browning too quickly, lower the temperature and let the oil cool slightly before frying any more. Use a slotted spoon to transfer the fried empanadas to the prepared rack to drain. Serve them immediately, or keep them warm in a 250°F (120°C) oven for up to 1 hour before serving.

NOTE: Once fried, these empanadas can be frozen for up to 3 months. Freeze them in a single layer on baking sheets lined with parchment paper; once frozen solid, they can be transferred to freezer boxes or zip-top bags. Reheat them at 350°F (175°C) for 12 to 15 minutes, or until their centers are hot.

FLAKY HEARTS OF PALM PILLOWS

++

★ PASTÉIS DE PALMITO ★ BRAZIL ★

Crispy and flaky pastry is a great backdrop for this creamy and tangy filling. Brazilians feature hearts of palm (also known as *palmitos*) enthusiastically in their cuisine. You'll find them used in salads, soups, and stews, and transformed into creams, such as the one that's hidden within these scrumptious empanadas. Hearts of palm are sold in jars or cans, packed in acidic brine. I prefer to purchase them in jars that actually allow me to see what I'm getting. My Brazilian friend, Janine, tells me that in Brazil, the hearts of palm are usually left in large chunks as to provide crunch but that my method produces a more elegant version of *pastéis*. I make this in a food processor, but you could just as easily chop everything by hand. Either way, you'll want to serve these immediately after making them so that they don't become soggy. Since hearts of palm can be salty, there is little need for added salt in this recipe.

++

MAKES **12** *PASTÉIS*

MAKE THE FILLING: In the bowl of a food processor fitted with a metal blade, combine the hearts of palm, white onion, and garlic. Pulse until they are finely chopped, about 6 one-second intervals, stopping to scrape the sides of the bowl as needed. Add the cream cheese, parsley, and green onions and pulse until combined, about 6 one-second intervals, stopping to scrape the sides of the bowl as needed. Transfer the hearts of palm mixture to a bowl and season it with the salt and pepper. Cover with plastic and chill the filling for at least 1 hour or up to overnight.

Continued ➡

1 (14½-ounce/410-g) jar hearts of palm, drained and sliced

½ cup (60 g) finely minced white onion

2 large cloves garlic, thinly sliced

4 ounces (115 g) cream cheese, softened to room temperature

2 tablespoons minced fresh Italian parsley (leaves and tender stems)

2 tablespoons minced green onions (white and light green parts)

½ teaspoon fine sea salt, or to taste

¼ teaspoon freshly ground black pepper, or to taste

1 recipe *Pastéis* Dough (page 33)

Vegetable oil for frying

ASSEMBLE THE *PASTÉIS*: After the filling chills, make the dough as directed on page 33 and let it rest, covered with plastic, for 20 minutes at room temperature. Line a large baking sheet with parchment paper; set it aside. Divide the dough in half. Roll out the first half to 1/16 inch (2 mm) thick (like for pasta). Using a pastry cutter or very sharp knife, cut it into 5-by-6-inch (12-by-15-cm) rectangles. Re-roll the scraps together, wrap them in the plastic, and allow them to rest for 20 minutes. In the meantime, repeat with the other half of the dough, cutting and re-rolling the scraps (while allowing the dough to rest in between), until you have 12 rectangles. You may have to do this a third time, until all are cut. The bottom side of the rectangles will be sticky; the top will be dry.

With a shorter side toward you and the sticky side facing up, place 2 tablespoons of the filling in the bottom half of each rectangle, leaving ½ inch (12 mm) all around. Fold the top over the filling and seal all of the sides well by pressing them together with your fingers. Crimp them shut with the tines of a fork. Transfer them to the prepared baking sheet.

FRY THE *PASTÉIS* AND SERVE: Fit a large baking sheet with a metal cooling rack; set it aside. In a large skillet with high sides, heat ½ to 1 inch (about 2 cm) of vegetable oil to 360°F (180°C) or use a deep-fryer according to the manufacturer's directions. Working in batches, carefully slide the *pastéis* into the oil. Fry them until they're puffy and golden, 1½ to 2 minutes, turning them over halfway though. If the oil gets too hot as you fry and they're browning too quickly, lower the temperature and let the oil cool slightly before frying any more. Remove them with a slotted spoon and place them on the prepared rack to drain. Let them cool for 1 to 2 minutes and serve.

NOTE: *Pastéis* are best fried immediately after shaping and eaten immediately after they're fried. Freeze them uncooked and uncovered in a single layer; once solid, transfer them to freezer bags and keep them frozen for up to 3 months. Fry them without thawing (to prevent splatters) for 3 to 3½ minutes, or until they are golden and crispy.

FRIED CASSAVA AND CHEESE TURNOVERS

★ EMPANADAS DE YUCA Y QUESO ★ CENTRAL AMERICA ★

1 recipe Cassava or Yuca Dough (page 28)

10 ounces (280 g) queso blanco or Monterey Jack cheese

Vegetable oil for frying

Salt for sprinkling

These tropical, gluten-free empanadas are crispy and chewy at the same time. As if that weren't enough deliciousness, they're filled with gooey queso blanco—a mild, white melting cheese, now being produced in the United States. Cassava (or yuca) has a taste reminiscent of potato, but sweeter. Processing it activates its starch content, making it gluey to work with. This is precisely what helps the dough to hold together when molded into empanadas. Although these empanadas may look flat when first assembled, they actually puff up during the cooking (and reheating) process. Keep your hands moist to shape the dough into balls, and use my tortilla-press method (see page 22) to produce these empanadas without much effort. I like to make several batches of these, which I fry and then freeze. I simply reheat as many as I want in a hot oven and serve them on their own, with chimichurri (page 162), or as a side dish to any roast or grilled meat and poultry. Purchase fresh or frozen, peeled, and sectioned yuca if you can, but stay away from the canned stuff, which is too mushy and won't work here.

MAKES 12 TO 14 EMPANADAS

ASSEMBLE THE EMPANADAS: Make the dough as directed on page 28 and let it rest, covered with plastic, for 30 minutes at room temperature.

Line a large baking sheet with parchment paper; set it aside. With moistened hands, divide the dough into 12 to 14 portions (about 2 ounces/55 g each). Moisten your hands again and shape them into small balls. Cut the cheese into slices measuring approximately 1½ by 2½ inches (4 by 6 cm) and ¼ inch (6 mm) thick. Line a tortilla press with a zip-top freezer bag that has been cut open on three sides like a book.

Continued ➤

Place a ball in the middle of the bag; flatten it slightly. Place the bag in the tortilla press and flatten the ball into a 4½-inch (11-cm) disc about ⅛ inch (3 mm) thick. If you don't have a tortilla press, use a flat-bottomed heavy skillet to press it down. Place one slice of cheese in the middle of the disc, leaving a small rim; use the bag to fold the dough over the filling, forming a half-moon. Press the edges together with your fingers to seal well. Transfer the empanada to the prepared sheet. Repeat with the rest of the dough and filling, keeping the empanadas covered as you go.

FRY THE EMPANADAS AND SERVE: Fit a large baking sheet with a metal cooling rack; set it aside. In a large skillet with high sides, heat 1 to 1½ inches (2.5 to 4 cm) of oil to 360°F (180°C) or use a deep-fryer according to the manufacturer's directions. Working in batches, carefully slide the empanadas into the oil. Fry them until they are golden, about 4 minutes, turning them over halfway through. If the oil gets too hot as you fry and they're browning too quickly, lower the temperature and let the oil cool slightly before frying any more. Use a slotted spoon to transfer the fried empanadas to the prepared rack to drain. Sprinkle them with salt, let them rest for 1 to 2 minutes, and serve.

> **NOTE:** To freeze after frying, cool the empanadas thoroughly and place them in a single layer on baking sheets. Freeze until solid; transfer them to freezer bags, and freeze for up to 4 months. Heat them in a 350°F (175°C) oven until heated through, 12 to 15 minutes.

LIGHT-AS-AIR ONION AND CHEESE PIES

+++

★ EMPANADAS DE VIENTO ★ ECUADOR ★

Addictive and sweet, these fried, elegant vegetarian morsels are native to Ecuador. They are crumbly and delicate, and are said to be made of air (*viento*). My variation includes a touch of leeks, which are sweeter in taste than onions. Their subtle flavor is magnified by a generous coating of crunchy sugar that turns these pastries into crispy and sweet delights. In Ecuador, they're just served by themselves as a snack. I like to serve them as part of a cheese tray composed of seasonal fruit; a mix of creamy, blue, and sharp cheeses; and quince or guava paste. Paired with a dessert wine or sparkling wine, they make an elegant end to any meal.

+++

MAKES 26 EMPANADAS

MAKE THE FILLING: In a medium nonstick pan, heat the olive oil over medium-high heat. Add the onions and leeks; sauté until they are softened, 2 to 3 minutes. Remove them from the heat and let them cool completely.

In a medium bowl, combine the onion mixture with the cheese. Chill the filling, covered, for at least 1 hour or overnight.

ASSEMBLE THE EMPANADAS: While the filling chills, make the dough as directed on page 29 and let it rest, covered with plastic or a damp towel, for 1 hour at room temperature.

Dust a clean surface with flour; roll out the pastry to ⅛ inch (3 mm) thick (like for piecrust). Use a 3¾-inch (9.5-cm) round cutter to cut 26 rounds, re-rolling the scraps as needed, until all the rounds are cut (see Notes). Keep the rounds covered

Continued ➡

2 teaspoons extra-virgin olive oil

1 cup (120 g) finely chopped white onions

1 cup (100 g) finely chopped leeks (white and light green parts only)

2¼ cups (270 g) grated queso fresco or Monterey Jack

1 recipe Master Dough (page 29)

Egg wash, made with 1 beaten egg and 2 teaspoons water

1 cup (200 g) sugar

Vegetable oil for frying

with a damp cloth as you work. Working with a few pastry rounds at a time, moisten the edges with the egg wash and place 1 tablespoon of the filling in the center of each round. Fold the top of the dough over the filling to form half-moon shapes. Press the edges with your fingers, then press them again with the tines of a fork to seal. It will be helpful to press out the air from the middle of the empanadas as you shape them, so that they don't puff up excessively as they fry. Set the empanadas on a baking sheet (keeping them covered with a clean kitchen towel as you work); refrigerate them uncovered for 1 hour.

FRY THE EMPANADAS AND SERVE: Fit a baking sheet with a metal cooling rack and set it aside. Place the sugar in a shallow bowl; set it aside.

In a Dutch oven, heat 2 inches (5 cm) of vegetable oil to 360°F (180°C). Or use a deep-fryer, according to the manufacturer's instructions. Fry the empanadas in batches until they're golden, 1½ to 2 minutes, turning them so that both sides cook. If the oil gets too hot as you fry and they're browning too quickly, lower the temperature and let the oil cool slightly before frying any more. Remove the empanadas with a slotted spoon and place them on the rack to drain; let them cool for 1 minute. While they are still warm, roll them in the sugar, coating all sides. Set them back on the rack; let them cool slightly before serving.

NOTES: The less you play with this dough, the more tender it will be, so I suggest you try to cut as many rounds as you possibly can from the first roll. Knead the scraps back together for 30 seconds (just until the dough holds back together), cover it with plastic or with a damp towel, and let it rest for 10 minutes before re-rolling. If the dough still shrinks as you roll it, step back, let it rest on the counter, covered, for 10 minutes, and then roll it out again. To get all of the rounds, you'll have to roll the dough very thinly.

These are best eaten fresh. You can shape the empanadas ahead of time and place them uncooked, in a single layer, on a baking sheet; freeze them until solid, then transfer them to bags and freeze them for up to 1 month. They can go directly from freezer to fryer without thawing. You'll need to fry them for about 3 minutes, or until crispy and golden. Roll them in the sugar and serve.

CHAPTER 3

★ ★

BEEF & PORK

EMPANADAS

BY FAR, MOST OF THE EMPANADAS IN LATIN AMERICA ARE FILLED WITH BEEF AND PORK, SO IT'S NO COINCIDENCE THAT THIS IS THE LONGEST CHAPTER IN THIS BOOK. In Argentina, Chile, and Uruguay (the heart of empanada territory), there are hundreds of recipes for beef empanadas. In Argentina alone, they vary by region, by city, and by household. Some are studded with raisins; others are splashed with vinegar; some are heavily dressed with sautéed onions; while others are made only with beef that has been minced by hand. Selecting which ones to include in this chapter in a way that reflects the entirety of the Latin American territory was no easy task. For this reason, rather than attempting to be comprehensive, I decided to select just my favorite recipes to include here. The recipes in this chapter won't disappoint. You'll find the famous envelope-shaped empanadas from Chile called *empanadas de pino*, and the cassava-crusted beef empanadas from the Dominican Republic called *cativias*.

Pork is another favored ingredient used to stuff empanadas. Many pork empanada renditions showcase the combination of sweet and savory flavors that were featured in the original empanadas that arrived with the Spanish colonizers centuries ago. They remain embedded in the empanada registry of Latin America. Among these are several that are encrusted with a generous coating of sugar so that every bite offers a bit of meat and a bit of sweetness. Depending on your mood (and your appetite), these empanadas can be served as part of a meal or as the appetizers before supper. These are the recipes that have made Latin American empanadas famous around the world. Enjoy them and share them with others, continuing to spread this love affair with the hand-held pies of the New World.

HAND-CUT BEEF, EGG, AND GREEN ONION EMPANADAS

+++

★ EMPANADAS TUCUMANAS ★ ARGENTINA ★

¼ cup (60 ml) extra-virgin olive oil

2 cups (240 g) finely chopped white onions

2 tablespoons smoked Spanish paprika (pimentón)

2½ teaspoons fine sea salt

2 teaspoons ground cumin

½ teaspoon red pepper flakes

½ teaspoon freshly ground black pepper

1 to 1¼ pounds (455 to 570 g) Cooked Flank Steak (page 18), finely diced

1½ cups (360 ml) beef broth (or cooking liquid from the flank)

1 tablespoon red wine vinegar

3 hard-boiled eggs (see page 15), peeled and finely chopped

¾ cup (50 g) thinly sliced green onions (white and light green parts)

1 recipe Bread Dough (page 30)

Egg wash, made with 1 beaten egg and 2 teaspoons water (optional)

There is an empanada competition held in Tucumán, Argentina, every year, in which several dozen competitors vie for the first prize of the Empanada de Oro. These large empanadas are stuffed with a mixture of tender beef that is moist and spicy. What makes these pies special is that the beef—usually flank steak—is first cooked and then diced by hand. This hand-cut beef is called *carne a cuchillo* ("knife-cut beef"), and cooks in this region of Argentina consider it a sacrilege to use ground beef. Plan to make this filling hours before assembling the empanadas (preferably the night before) so that the juices in the filling have time to thicken in the refrigerator. Once baked, these empanadas will be moist inside but not soupy. Traditional Tucumán empanadas are not brushed with egg wash and have a matte look; I prefer them shiny and like to use it.

+++

MAKES 28 EMPANADAS

MAKE THE FILLING: Heat the oil in a large skillet with high sides over medium-high heat. Add the white onions and cook, stirring, until softened, about 5 minutes. Add the paprika, salt, cumin, red pepper flakes, and black pepper, stirring well to combine. Add the beef and broth, stirring to combine. Bring them to a boil; lower the heat to medium and continue cooking, uncovered, until all of the liquid has been absorbed, about 10 minutes (the beef mixture should be moist). Remove the filling from the heat and stir in the vinegar; cover and chill the filling completely, at least 3 hours (preferably overnight).

Continued ➔

ASSEMBLE THE EMPANADAS: After the filling chills, make the dough as directed on page 30 and let it rest, covered with plastic wrap, for 10 minutes at room temperature. Divide the dough into 28 equal pieces (about 2 ounces/55 g each). Roll each piece into a ball, folding the bottom of the dough onto itself so that the ends are at the bottom and the tops are smooth (the way you'd shape rolls). Place them on a lightly floured baking sheet and cover them with a clean towel; let them rest for 10 minutes. On a well-floured surface, press each ball slightly into a flat disc. Line a tortilla press with a zip-top freezer bag that has been cut open on three sides so that it opens like a book. Place a disc in the middle of the tortilla press and flatten it into a 5-inch (12-cm) round, ⅛ inch (3 mm) thick (or roll it out with a rolling pin). Stack the discs with parchment paper in between to avoid sticking.

Stir the eggs and green onions into the filling. Place 2 heaping tablespoons of the filling in the center of each empanada. Fold the bottom of the dough to meet the top of the disc, encasing the filling and forming a half-moon, and press the edges together well. Make ½-inch (12-mm) edges by pressing the rims between your fingers using the *repulgue* method (see page 31). The empanadas can sit uncovered at room temperature for 20 minutes before baking or can be refrigerated for up to 1 hour before baking.

BAKE THE EMPANADAS AND SERVE: Preheat the oven to 450°F (230°C). Line three baking sheets with parchment paper. Place the empanadas on the prepared pans and brush them with the egg wash, if using. Bake them for 28 to 30 minutes, until their bottoms are golden (rotate the pans in the oven halfway through baking, back to front and top to bottom, to ensure that all of the empanadas bake evenly). Transfer the empanadas to a cooling rack; let them cool for 3 to 5 minutes before serving.

NOTE: To freeze these empanadas, cool them to room temperature; set them in a single layer on a baking sheet and freeze them until solid. When solid, transfer them to zip-top bags or freezer boxes and freeze them for up to 4 months. Reheat them in a 350°F (175°C) oven until warmed through, 10 to 15 minutes.

FAMOUS BEEF, RAISIN, AND OLIVE HAND PIES

+++

★ EMPANADAS DE PINO ★ CHILE ★

These empanadas are sweet, briny, meaty, and a meal unto themselves. Unlike their Argentinean counterparts (see page 66), they're folded into rustic packages that resemble envelopes and don't have intricately shaped borders. This whimsical way of shaping them has made them famous around the world. Their crusts are painted with an egg and milk wash that lacquers them, making them very shiny. In Chile, the beef (*pino*) is traditionally minced by hand. I find it easier to shape these empanadas one at a time, so I roll, fill, and shape consecutively until I'm done with all of them (as opposed to shaping the discs first). Serve these alone or with a side of Red Pepper Salsa (page 164).

+++

MAKES 22 EMPANADAS

MAKE THE FILLING: In a large skillet, heat the oil over medium-high heat. Add the onions; cook until they start to turn golden, 6 to 7 minutes. Add the garlic and cook for 20 seconds. Add the paprika, cumin, salt, oregano, and pepper; stir well. Add the beef and raisins; cook for 2 minutes. Add ½ cup (120 ml) water (or cooking liquid from the steak) and simmer it for 30 seconds, or until the liquid is absorbed. Remove the filling from the heat; transfer it to a large plate and let it cool for 30 minutes. Cover and chill it for at least 2 hours or overnight.

ASSEMBLE THE EMPANADAS: After the filling chills, make the dough as directed on page 30 and let it rest, covered with plastic or with a damp towel, for 10 minutes at room temperature. Divide the dough into 22 equal pieces (about 2¾ ounces/75 g each). Roll each piece into a ball, folding the bottom of

Continued ➡

¼ cup (60 ml) olive oil

2 cups (240 g) finely chopped yellow onions

3 large cloves garlic, minced

1 tablespoon smoked Spanish paprika (pimentón)

1½ teaspoons ground cumin

1½ teaspoons fine sea salt

1 teaspoon dried oregano

¼ teaspoon freshly ground black pepper

2 pounds (910 g) Cooked Flank Steak (page 18), finely diced

½ cup (85 g) golden raisins

22 whole pitted green or Manzanilla olives

6 hard-boiled eggs (see page 15), peeled and quartered

1 egg white, beaten

1 recipe Bread Dough (page 30)

Egg wash, made with 1 beaten egg and 2 teaspoons half-and-half or milk

the dough onto itself so that the ends are at the bottom and the tops are smooth (the way you'd shape rolls). Place them on a lightly floured baking sheet and cover them with a clean towel; let them rest for 10 minutes. On a well-floured surface, press each ball slightly into a flat disc.

Line a tortilla press with a zip-top freezer bag that has been cut open on three sides so that it opens like a book. Place a disc in the middle of the tortilla press and flatten it into a 6½-inch (16.5-cm) round, about ⅛ inch (3 mm) thick (or roll it out with a rolling pin). Stack the discs with parchment paper in between to avoid sticking.

Line three baking sheets with parchment paper; set them aside. Place ¼ cup (60 ml) of the filling, one-quarter of an egg, and an olive in the bottom half of a disc, leaving a ½-inch (12-mm) rim without filling. Fold the bottom of the dough to meet the top of the disc, encasing the filling and forming a half-moon, and press the edges together well. Flatten it to make a 1-inch (2.5-cm) rim all around; brush the top of the rim with some of the egg white. Fold the side rims toward the middle of the empanada; fold the top rim toward the middle (like an envelope). Repeat with the remaining dough and fillings, until all the ingredients are used. The empanadas can sit uncovered at room temperature for 20 minutes before baking, or can be refrigerated for up to 1 hour before baking.

BAKE THE EMPANADAS AND SERVE: Preheat the oven to 400°F (205°C). Place the empanadas on the prepared pans and brush them with the egg wash. Bake the empanadas for 28 to 30 minutes, until their tops are golden (rotate the pans in the oven halfway through baking, back to front and top to bottom, to ensure that all of the empanadas bake evenly). Transfer the empanadas to a cooling rack. Let them rest for 3 to 5 minutes. Serve them hot or at room temperature.

> **NOTE:** To freeze these empanadas, cool them to room temperature; set them in a single layer on a baking sheet and freeze them until solid. When solid, transfer them to zip-top bags or freezer boxes and freeze them for up to 4 months. Reheat them in a 350°F (175°C) oven until warmed through, 12 to 15 minutes.

GOLDEN AND JUICY BEEF AND POTATO PIES

+++

★ SALTEÑAS DE CARNE ★ BOLIVIA ★

1 tablespoon unflavored gelatin

2 cups (480 ml) cold low-sodium beef broth

2 tablespoons vegetable oil

1 cup (120 g) finely chopped white onions

1 cup (100 g) finely chopped green bell peppers

1 tablespoon sweet smoked Spanish paprika (pimentón)

1 tablespoon annatto paste (achiote) or Bijol (see Notes on page 40)

2 cups (260 g) peeled and finely chopped Yukon gold potatoes

1 pound (455 g) tri-tip or flat-iron steak, finely chopped

1 cup (120 g) green peas

½ cup (20 g) finely chopped fresh parsley (tender stems and leaves)

1 tablespoon sugar

2 teaspoons fine sea salt

1½ teaspoons ground cumin

1 teaspoon dried oregano

¼ teaspoon freshly ground black pepper

1 recipe *Salteña* Dough (page 32)

Egg wash, made with 1 beaten egg and 1 tablespoon water

In Bolivia, there are festivals entirely dedicated to *salteñas*, where bakers vie for the coveted first prize. Among what judges look for are the color of the dough—which should be from a golden yellow to a bright orange hue—and the juiciness of the stew, which in some cases runs down your arms. The juicier they are, the harder they are to make. This version is moist, but not too juicy. Beef *salteñas* are the most traditional of these football-shaped pies. The proper way to eat them is to first bite off one of the corners, then add a dash of hot sauce and drink the juices that flow out. Take care not to crowd the *salteñas* on the baking sheets, or they'll stick together, causing the juices to ooze out.

++

MAKES 26 TO 28 *SALTEÑAS*

MAKE THE FILLING: In a large, heat-resistant glass bowl, combine the gelatin and broth; stir to mix it together and let it sit for 2 minutes. Heat the gelatin mixture in the microwave on high for 1½ minutes, until the gelatin is dissolved (or over medium-low heat in a double boiler for 3 to 4 minutes); set aside.

Heat the oil in a large skillet over medium-high heat. Add the onions and bell peppers; cook until they are softened, 3 to 4 minutes. Add the paprika and annatto or Bijol; cook for 30 seconds. Add the broth mixture, stirring until the spices are dissolved. Add the potatoes, beef, peas, parsley, sugar, salt, cumin, oregano, and black pepper; bring the liquid to a boil and cook, uncovered, until the potatoes are tender, about 6 minutes. Transfer the stew to a medium bowl and set it over a large bowl of iced water to cool it quickly. Cool the stew completely; cover it with plastic wrap and chill it for at least 6 hours or overnight (the mixture will jell).

Continued ➡

ASSEMBLE THE *SALTEÑAS*: After the filling chills, make the dough as directed on page 32 and let it rest, covered with plastic or with a damp towel, for 45 to 60 minutes at room temperature.

Dust two baking sheets with flour; set them aside. Divide the dough into 26 to 28 equal portions (about 3 ounces/85 g each). Roll each piece into a ball, folding the bottom of the dough onto itself so that the ends are at the bottom and the tops are smooth (the way you'd shape rolls). Place them on a prepared baking sheet and cover them with a clean towel; let them rest for 20 minutes.

Line two baking sheets with parchment paper; set them aside. Working one at a time on a lightly floured surface, flatten each ball slightly into a disc. Line a tortilla press with a zip-top freezer bag that has been cut open on three sides so that it opens like a book. Place the disc in the middle of the tortilla press and press the dough into a 6-inch (15-cm) disc, about ⅛ inch (3 mm) thick (or roll it out with a rolling pin). Stack the discs with parchment paper in between to avoid sticking.

Place 3 heaping tablespoons of the jelled filling in the middle of the disc; bring the edges of the pastry together, letting the dough stretch over the filling. Enclose the filling (press the filling down with your forefinger to compact it). Form a half-moon and, holding it by the top edges, stand the *salteña* on its bottom, flattening it so it can stand without toppling. Pinch the edges tightly, and press to form a small rim, about ½ inch (12 mm) wide. Then pinch and fold sections of the rim decoratively to seal it well (as you would a dumpling, by gathering the dough starting at one end and pressing it together at ½-inch (12-mm) intervals, until it's all sealed). Stand the *salteñas* on the prepared pans and chill them for at least 20 minutes (or up to 2 hours).

BAKE THE *SALTEÑAS* AND SERVE: Preheat the oven to 425°F (220°C). Brush the *salteñas* with the egg wash. Bake them for 35 to 40 minutes, or until they are golden (rotate the pans in the oven halfway through baking, back to front and top to bottom, to ensure that all of the empanadas bake evenly). Transfer the *salteñas* to a cooling rack. Let them cool for 5 to 10 minutes before serving.

NOTE: To freeze the *salteñas*, cool them thoroughly after baking in a single layer. Freeze them until solid. Store them in containers for up to 4 months; reheat them in a 350°F (175°C) oven until hot, 15 to 20 minutes.

SWEET PLANTAIN
AND BEEF TURNOVERS

✦✦

★ **EMPANADAS DE MADUROS Y PICADILLO** ★ **CENTRAL AMERICA** ★

Sweet plantains surround spicy beef filling in these empanadas that Central Americans call *pasteles*. Others in Latin America know them as *empanadas de maduros* (ripe plantain empanadas). The filling is seasoned heavily and contrasts with the sweetness of the dough. Serve these with crema, Avocado Salsa (page 167), or Red Pepper Salsa (page 164). Make these for brunch, as they pair deliciously with eggs; they're also great with a side of rice and beans. You will need a food processor to make this recipe.

✦✦✦

MAKES 12 EMPANADAS

MAKE THE FILLING: Place the onions, bell peppers, tomatoes, jalapeño or serrano pepper, and garlic in the bowl of a food processor fitted with a metal blade; process until smooth. In a large skillet, heat the olive oil over medium-high heat; add the processed mixture and cook until it is thickened, 2 to 3 minutes. Add the beef, breaking it down with the back of the spoon until it's no longer pink, 3 to 4 minutes. Add the tomato paste, salt, oregano, and cumin and cook for 1 to 2 minutes. Reduce the heat to low; cook, stirring, for 5 minutes, or until slightly thickened. Let the filling cool completely; cover and chill it for at least 1 hour or overnight.

ASSEMBLE THE EMPANADAS: After the filling chills, make the dough as directed on page 35. Use immediately. Divide the dough into 12 equal portions (about 2 ounces/55 g each). With moistened hands, roll each into a ball, keeping them covered as you work. Line a tortilla press with a zip-top freezer bag that has been cut open on three sides so that it opens like a book. Place a ball of

Continued ➡

1 cup (120 g) roughly chopped white onions

1 cup (100 g) roughly chopped red bell peppers

½ cup (90 g) seeded and roughly chopped plum tomatoes

2 tablespoons minced jalapeño or serrano pepper (seeded and deveined if less heat is desired)

2 large cloves garlic, roughly chopped

2 tablespoons extra-virgin olive oil

¾ pound (340 g) lean ground beef

2 tablespoons tomato paste

2 teaspoons fine sea salt

1 teaspoon dried oregano (preferably Mexican)

1 teaspoon ground cumin

1 recipe Sweet Plantain Dough (page 35)

Vegetable oil for frying

⅓ cup (40 g) all-purpose flour (or rice flour or chickpea flour for gluten-free)

dough in the middle of the tortilla press and flatten it into a 5½-inch (14-cm) disc about ⅛ inch (3 mm) thick. If you don't have a tortilla press, use a flat-bottomed, heavy skillet to press it down.

Line two baking sheets with parchment paper; set them aside. Place 2 heaping tablespoons of the filling in the middle of the disc, leaving a ½-inch (12-mm) rim; use the bag to fold the dough over the filling, forming a half-moon. Press the edges together with your fingers to seal well. Place the empanada on a prepared pan. Repeat with the rest of the dough and filling, keeping the empanadas covered as you go.

FRY THE EMPANADAS AND SERVE: Fit a large baking sheet with a metal cooling rack set it aside. In a large skillet with high sides, heat ½ to 1 inch (12 mm to 2.5 cm) of oil to 350°F (175°C) or use a deep-fryer according to the manufacturer's directions. Working in batches, dredge the empanadas in the flour and slide them into the vegetable oil. Fry them until they are golden and crispy, 3 to 4 minutes, turning them over halfway through. If the oil gets too hot as you fry and they're browning too quickly, lower the temperature and cool the oil slightly before frying any more (see Notes). Use a slotted spoon to transfer the fried empanadas to the prepared rack to drain. Let them rest for 1 to 2 minutes before serving.

NOTES: This dough is simple to make but you must keep a close eye on empanadas made with plantains as they fry, as their high sugar content can cause the dough to burn. Since all of the ingredients are already cooked, all that is needed is to sear the exteriors, which will help the sweet plantains caramelize into golden deliciousness. Dredging the empanadas in flour lightly before frying them prevents them from sticking to the bottom of the pan as they fry.

It is best to make the empanadas the day they are to be served. To freeze, let the fried empanadas cool and place them on a baking sheet in a single layer. Freeze until solid; transfer them to freezer containers and freeze them for up to 2 months. Bake, without thawing, in a 400°F (205°C) oven for 10 to 15 minutes, or until hot.

BEEF AND DRIED CHILE MASA PIES

+++

★ EMPANADAS DE CARNE Y SALSA DE CHILES ★ MEXICO ★

3 dried ancho chiles

3 dried guajillo chiles

Boiling water

2 large cloves garlic, minced

1 teaspoon fine sea salt

½ teaspoon freshly ground black pepper

1½ pounds (680 g) Cooked Flank Steak (page 18), finely shredded

1 recipe Masa Dough (page 24)

Vegetable oil for frying

Shredded iceberg lettuce for garnish

Seeded and chopped plum tomatoes for garnish

2 Hass avocados, finely chopped

2 cups (480 ml) Mexican crema or sour cream

1 cup (100 g) crumbled queso seco or grated pecorino Romano

1 recipe Dried Chile, Bell Pepper, and Tomato Sauce (page 169)

In Mexico, stuff raw masa with cheese, fold it in half, seal the edges, cook it, and you've got a quesadilla (unlike their American counterparts that are made by sandwiching two tortillas with cheese). But stuff masa with any other filling and it's called an empanada, even if it looks and cooks exactly the same way. These are stuffed with sauced-up shredded beef and garnished with a colorful potpourri of toppings. A little bit of the sauce added to the masa gives it a red hue. Dried chiles are easy to find in most grocery stores (see Sources, page 172). Serve these empanadas with plenty of toppings and Dried Chile, Bell Pepper, and Tomato Sauce (page 169).

+++

MAKES 12 EMPANADAS

MAKE THE FILLING: Place the ancho and guajillo chiles in a medium bowl and cover them with boiling water (set a heavy plate on top to keep them submerged). Soak the chiles for 15 minutes; remove them from the water with tongs and reserve 1 cup (240 ml) of the soaking liquid (discard the rest). Make a slit in each chile and remove the stem, seeds, and veins. Place the chiles in a blender and pour ½ cup (120 ml) of the soaking liquid over them; add the garlic and blend until smooth, adding more of the soaking liquid as needed (1 tablespoon at a time) to make ½ cup (120 ml) of thick paste. Transfer the chile paste to a small bowl; season it with the salt and pepper. Add ¼ cup (60 ml) of the paste to the beef and stir well; cover and chill it for 1 hour (or overnight). Cover the remaining paste and refrigerate until needed (up to 2 days).

Continued ➜

ASSEMBLE THE EMPANADAS: After the filling chills, make the dough as directed on page 24, adding ¼ cup (60 ml) of the chile paste to the dough. Knead it well, until the masa has uniformly taken on a red hue, and let it rest, covered with plastic or with a damp towel, for 10 minutes at room temperature.

Line a baking sheet with parchment paper and set it aside. Line a tortilla press with a zip-top freezer bag that has been cut open on three sides so that it opens like a book. Divide the masa into 12 equal portions (about 2½ ounces/70 g each). Roll each portion into a ball and keep them covered with a damp kitchen towel as you work. Place a ball of masa in the middle of the tortilla press and flatten it into a 5½-inch (14-cm) disc about ⅛ inch (3 mm) thick. If you don't have a tortilla press, use a flat-bottomed, heavy skillet to press the dough. Place 2 heaping tablespoons of the filling in the middle of the empanada, leaving a small rim. Use the bag to fold the masa over the filling, forming a half-moon. Press the edges together with your fingers to seal. Transfer the empanada to the prepared baking sheet. Repeat with the rest of the dough and filling, keeping the empanadas covered as you go.

FRY THE EMPANADAS AND SERVE: Fit a large baking sheet with a metal cooling rack; set it aside. In a large skillet with high sides, heat 1 to 1½ inches (2.5 to 4 cm) of oil to 360°F (180°C) or use a deep-fryer according to the manufacturer's directions. Working in batches, carefully slide the empanadas into the oil. Fry them until golden, 4 to 6 minutes, turning them over halfway through. If the oil gets too hot as you fry and they're browning too quickly, lower the temperature and let the oil cool slightly before frying any more. Use a slotted spoon to transfer the fried empanadas to the prepared rack to drain. Serve the empanadas warm, topped with lettuce, tomatoes, avocados, crema or sour cream, cheese, and sauce.

NOTE: These empanadas are best eaten right after frying them. Once fried, these can be frozen for up to 4 months. Freeze them in a single layer on baking sheets lined with parchment paper; once frozen solid, transfer them to containers and freeze. Reheat them at 350°F (175°C) until their centers are warm, 15 to 20 minutes.

CUMIN SHREDDED BEEF EMPANADAS

✦✦✦

★ EMPANADAS DE CARNE MECHADA ★ VENEZUELA ★

These crispy corn empanadas are filled with succulent shredded beef. There are many recipes for shredded beef in Latin America, but the taste of cumin is what most distinguishes the *carne mechada* of Venezuela. In Sucre, it's made with Worcestershire sauce and tomato paste, and in the state of Nueva Esparta, it's often flavored with leeks and green onions. This version is one of my favorite recipes and is based on the empanadas served in Caracas. This style of cooked beef is an important ingredient in their national dish called *pabellón,* which also contains black beans, rice, and sweet plantains. More often than not, these empanadas are made with leftovers from a previous meal. I like to serve these with a side of Avocado Salsa (page 167), but they are just as succulent paired with a simple lettuce, onion, and tomato salad.

✦✦✦✦✦✦✦✦✦✦✦✦✦✦✦✦✦✦✦✦✦✦✦✦✦✦✦✦✦✦✦✦✦✦✦✦✦✦✦

MAKES 20 EMPANADAS

MAKE THE FILLING: Heat the olive oil in a medium nonstick pan over medium-high heat. Add the onion and bell pepper; cook for 2 minutes, or until they're softened. Add the tomatoes, garlic, salt, black pepper, and cumin. Cook for 1 to 2 minutes, until the mixture begins to thicken. Add the beef and broth; stir well to combine. Cook for 3 to 4 minutes, until most of the liquid has been absorbed. Stir in the parsley, remove the filling from the heat, and let it cool completely. Cover and chill it for at least 2 hours or overnight.

ASSEMBLE THE EMPANADAS: After the filling chills, make the dough as directed on page 26 and let it rest, covered with plastic or with a damp towel, for 10 minutes at room temperature.

Continued ➤

1 tablespoon olive oil

½ cup (60 g) minced yellow onion

¼ cup (30 g) minced red bell pepper

½ cup (90 g) seeded and minced plum tomatoes

2 large cloves garlic, minced

1 teaspoon fine sea salt

½ teaspoon freshly ground black pepper

½ teaspoon ground cumin

1 to 1¼ pounds (455 to 570 g) shredded Cooked Flank Steak (page 18)

1 cup (240 ml) reserved broth from cooking the steak or low-sodium beef broth

2 tablespoons minced fresh Italian parsley (leaves and tender stems)

1 recipe Cornmeal Dough (page 26)

Vegetable oil for frying

Line two baking sheets with parchment paper; set them aside. Divide the dough into 20 equal pieces (about 2½ ounces/70 g each). Line a tortilla press with a zip-top freezer bag that has been cut open on three sides so that it opens like a book. Place a ball of dough in the middle of the tortilla press and flatten it into a 5-inch (12-cm) round, about ⅛ inch (3 mm) thick (see Notes). If you don't have a tortilla press, flatten each ball using a flat-bottomed, heavy skillet.

Place 2 heaping tablespoons of the filling in the middle of the round, leaving a small rim. Use the bag to fold the dough over the filling, forming a half-moon. Press the edges together with your fingers to seal. Transfer the empanada to a prepared baking sheet. Repeat with the rest of the dough and filling, keeping the empanadas covered as you go. These empanadas can be shaped and filled up to 1 hour before frying as long as you keep them covered and chilled until you're ready to fry.

FRY THE EMPANADAS AND SERVE: Fit a large baking sheet with a metal cooling rack and set it aside. In a large skillet with high sides, heat 1 to 1½ inches (2.5 to 4 cm) of vegetable oil to 360°F (180°C). You may also use a deep-fryer according to the manufacturer's directions. Working in batches of 4 or 5 empanadas at a time, carefully slide them into the oil. Fry them until golden, 3 to 4 minutes, turning them over halfway through. If the oil gets too hot as you fry and they're browning too quickly, lower the temperature and let the oil cool slightly before frying any more. Use a slotted spoon to transfer the fried empanadas to the prepared rack to drain. Serve them immediately, or keep them warm in a 250°F (120°C) oven for up to 1 hour before serving.

NOTES: Some cooks prefer to roll the dough into thicker discs, which yield a meatier texture. I like mine rolled somewhat thin because they produce crispier empanadas. To do so, my tortilla press method (see page 22) is particularly essential but you can experiment with different methods and thicknesses to find your favorite.

Once fried, these empanadas can be frozen for up to 3 months. Freeze them in a single layer on baking sheets lined with parchment paper; once frozen solid, they can be transferred to containers. Reheat them at 350°F (175°C) for 12 to 15 minutes, or until their centers are hot.

RAVIOLI-SHAPED PIES WITH STIR-FRIED BEEF, ONIONS, AND PEPPERS

★ EMPANADAS DE LOMO SALTADO ★ PERU ★

1 pound (455 g) beef tenderloin or flat-iron steak, cut into thin strips (2 by ½ inch/5 cm by 12 mm)

4 tablespoons (60 ml) vegetable oil

3 cups (360 g) thin strips white onions

2 cups (185 g) thin strips red bell peppers

1 cup (185 g) thin strips seeded Roma tomatoes

2 tablespoons soy sauce

1½ teaspoons fine sea salt

½ teaspoon freshly ground black pepper

½ cup (20 g) roughly chopped fresh cilantro (leaves and tender stems)

⅓ cup (20 g) thinly sliced bias-cut green onions

1 recipe Bread Dough (page 30)

1 large egg white, beaten

Egg wash, made with 1 beaten egg yolk and 2 teaspoons half-and-half or milk

Lomo saltado is the most famous stir-fried beef of Peru, where Asian culinary traditions permeate the cuisine. The beef—usually from the tenderloin—is traditionally seasoned with soy sauce (Peruvians call it *sillao*) and served over white rice, with a hefty addition of French fries. Recently, however, it has also become a filling for large, comforting, ravioli-shaped empanadas such as these. Serve them alone or as part of a meal with a side of fries and a tomato salad. Peruvian eateries often have two or three different hot sauces to serve with empanadas. My favorite is the Yellow Pepper Aioli (page 170), so I always serve it on the side, but your favorite hot sauces will work great too.

++

MAKES **14** EMPANADAS

MAKE THE FILLING: Pat the beef dry with paper towels. Heat 1 tablespoon of the oil in a large, nonstick sauté pan over medium-high heat. Add half of the beef and cook, stirring, until it is seared, 2 to 3 minutes. Remove it to a plate. Add another 1 tablespoon of the oil and repeat with the remaining beef; set it aside. Add the remaining 2 tablespoons oil and, when hot, add the white onions and bell peppers. Cook while stirring until they begin to soften but are still crisp, 2½ to 3 minutes. Add the tomatoes and soy sauce and cook for 2 minutes, or until most of the liquid is absorbed. Remove from the heat; add the beef and stir well. Season it with the salt and black pepper; cool it slightly and stir in the cilantro and green onions. Cover and chill the filling for at least 2 hours or overnight.

ASSEMBLE THE EMPANADAS: After the filling chills, make the dough as directed on page 30 and let it rest, covered with plastic or with a damp towel, for 10 minutes at room temperature.

Continued ➡

Divide the dough into 28 equal pieces (about 2 ounces/55 g each). Roll each piece into a ball, folding the bottom of the dough onto itself so that the ends are at the bottom and the tops are smooth (the way you'd shape rolls). Place them on a lightly floured baking sheet and cover them with a clean towel. Let them rest for 10 minutes. On a well-floured surface, press each ball slightly into a flat disc. Line a tortilla press with a zip-top freezer bag that has been cut open on three sides so that it opens like a book. Place a disc in the middle of the bag and flatten it slightly. Place the dough in the middle of the tortilla press and flatten it into a 5-inch (12-cm) round, about ⅛ inch (3 mm) thick (or roll it out with a rolling pin). Stack the discs with parchment paper in between to avoid sticking.

Line two baking sheets with parchment paper; set them aside. Working with one disc at a time, brush the edges with the egg white and center a heaping ¼ cup (60 ml) of the filling on it. Top with a second disc; the elastic dough will stretch over the filling until the edges of both discs meet. Press down the edges to form a 1-inch (2.5-cm) rim. Use your index finger and thumb to roll and pinch sections of the dough along the rim at ½-inch (12-mm) intervals to form a decorative (rustic) edge. Transfer the empanada to a prepared baking sheet. Repeat with the remaining dough and fillings, until all the ingredients are used. The empanadas can sit uncovered at room temperature for 20 minutes before baking or can be refrigerated for up to 1 hour before baking.

BAKE THE EMPANADAS AND SERVE: Preheat the oven to 400°F (205°C). Brush the empanadas with the egg wash. Bake them for 30 to 35 minutes, or until their bottoms are golden (rotate the pans in the oven halfway through baking, back to front and top to bottom, to ensure that all of the empanadas bake evenly). Transfer the empanadas to a cooling rack. Let them rest for 3 to 5 minutes before serving.

NOTE: After baking, cool and then freeze the empanadas in a single layer until solid; transfer them to zip-top bags or freezer boxes. Freeze them for up to 3 months. To reheat, place them in a 350°F (175°C) oven for about 15 minutes, or until heated through.

FLAKY GROUND BEEF AND HERB PILLOWS

+++

★ PASTÉIS DE CARNE MOIDA ★ BRAZIL ★

My next-door neighbor, Janine Hertzog Santos, is from the town of Porto Alegre in the state of Rio Grande do Sul, Brazil. We talked at length about the empanada tradition in her country and she was the inspiration for the *pastéis* recipes in this book. Not surprisingly, I trekked over to her house with freshly made *pastéis* so she could try them. She told me these reminded her of her mother's. Nothing could have made me happier! These are very similar to the *pastéis* made in the outdoor fairs in Brazil, with the exception that they're a bit smaller. Make sure to roll out the dough very thinly so that it will blister when it fries; that will ensure that they are crispy and brittle. In Brazil, these are often served with a light tomato salad. I like to eat them with Red Pepper Salsa (page 164) and a cold beer.

++

MAKES **12** *PASTÉIS*

MAKE THE FILLING: In a large, nonstick pan, heat 2 teaspoons of the oil over medium-high heat. Add the white onion and garlic and cook for 1 minute. Add the beef and brown it, breaking up the meat with the back of a spoon, until it's no longer pink, 2 to 3 minutes. Add ½ cup (120 ml) water and lower the heat to medium-low. Cook until most of the liquid is absorbed, 7 to 8 minutes. Fit a strainer on a bowl and drain the beef mixture; discard the liquid. Put the beef in the bowl and stir in the parsley, green onions, salt, and pepper. Cover the filling with plastic wrap and chill it for at least 1 hour or overnight.

ASSEMBLE THE *PASTÉIS*: After the filling chills, make the dough as directed on page 33 and let it rest, covered with plastic or with a damp towel, for 20 minutes at room temperature.

Continued ➜

2 teaspoons vegetable oil, plus more for frying

⅓ cup (40 g) finely chopped white onion

4 large cloves garlic, minced

¾ pound (340 g) lean ground beef

2 tablespoons finely chopped fresh Italian parsley (tender stems and leaves)

2 tablespoons finely chopped green onions

1 teaspoon fine sea salt, or to taste

¼ teaspoon freshly ground black pepper, or to taste

1 recipe *Pastéis* Dough (page 33)

Fit a large baking sheet with parchment paper; set it aside. Divide the dough in half. Roll out the first half to ⅟₁₆ inch (2 mm) thick (like for pasta). Using a pastry cutter or very sharp knife, cut it into 5-by-6-inch (12-by-15-cm) rectangles. Re-roll the scraps together, wrap them in the plastic, and allow them to rest for 20 minutes. In the meantime, repeat with the other half of the dough, cutting and re-rolling the scraps (while allowing the dough to rest in between), until you have 12 rectangles. You may have to do this a third time, until all are cut. The bottom side of the rectangles will be sticky; the top should be dry.

With a shorter side toward you and the sticky side facing up, place 2 tablespoons of the filling in the bottom half of each rectangle, leaving ½ inch (12 mm) all around. Fold the top over the filling and seal all of the sides well by pressing them together with your fingers. Crimp them tightly with the tines of a fork. Transfer them to the prepared baking sheet.

FRY THE *PASTÉIS* AND SERVE: Fit a large baking sheet with a metal cooling rack; set it aside. In a large skillet with high sides, heat ½ to 1 inch (about 2 cm) of oil to 360°F (180°C) or use a deep-fryer according to the manufacturer's directions. Working in batches, carefully slide the *pastéis* into the oil. Fry them until they're puffy and golden, 1½ to 2 minutes, turning them over halfway through. If the oil gets too hot as you fry and they're browning too quickly, lower the temperature and let the oil cool slightly before frying any more. Remove them with a slotted spoon and place them on the prepared rack to drain. Let them cool for 1 to 2 minutes and serve.

NOTE: *Pastéis* are best fried immediately after shaping and eaten immediately after they're fried. You can freeze them uncooked, in a single layer; once solid, transfer them to freezer bags and keep them frozen for up to 3 months. Fry them without thawing (to prevent splatters) for 3 to 3½ minutes, or until they are golden and crispy.

CRISPY CASSAVA AND BEEF EMPANADAS

+++

★ CATIVIAS ★ DOMINICAN REPUBLIC ★

1 cup (120 g) roughly chopped white onions

1 cup (85 g) roughly chopped leeks (white and light green parts only)

½ cup (90 g) seeded and roughly chopped plum tomatoes

½ cup (20 g) roughly chopped fresh Italian parsley

4 large cloves garlic, roughly chopped

1 tablespoon tomato paste

½ pound (225 g) lean ground beef

1 teaspoon fine sea salt, plus more for sprinkling

½ teaspoon freshly ground black pepper

1 tablespoon vegetable oil, plus more for frying

1 recipe Cassava or Yuca Dough (page 28)

These rich empanadas, called *cativias,* have a crunchy exterior and a deliciously chewy texture that marries beautifully with the beef filling hidden inside. They taste like crispy hash browns stuffed with beef. Cassava has a flavor reminiscent of potatoes, but its flesh renders a sturdier texture that holds its shape when fried; its subtle sweetness makes these little pies impossible to resist. They are among my husband's favorite empanadas. Ordinarily, cassava (or yuca) dough is extremely sticky and difficult to shape; my tortilla press method (see page 22) solves that problem. These empanadas must be fried as soon as they're shaped, but freeze beautifully and are easy to reheat. I make several batches at a time and keep them in my freezer. On busy nights, I'll reheat as many as I want. I recommend using a food processor to make these empanadas.

+++

MAKES 12 TO 14 EMPANADAS

MAKE THE FILLING: Place the onions, leeks, tomatoes, parsley, garlic, and tomato paste in the bowl of a food processor fitted with a metal blade; pulse until the mixture is smooth (about 15 one-second intervals), stopping to scrape down the sides of the bowl as needed. Add the beef, salt, and pepper and process until all is combined (8 to 10 one-second intervals), stopping to scrape down the sides of the bowl as needed.

Heat 1 tablespoon of the oil in a medium nonstick skillet over medium-high heat. Add the meat mixture and cook, breaking it down with a spoon, until it is no longer pink and all of the liquid has evaporated, 7 to 8 minutes. Remove the filling from the heat and let it cool completely. Transfer it to a bowl; cover and chill the filling for at least 1 hour or overnight.

Continued ➡

ASSEMBLE THE EMPANADAS: After the filling is chilled, make the dough as directed on page 28 and let it rest, covered with plastic or with a damp towel, for 30 minutes at room temperature.

Line two large baking sheets with parchment paper; set them aside. With moistened hands, divide the dough into 12 to 14 portions (about 2 ounces/55 g each). Moisten your hands again and shape them into small balls. Line a tortilla press with a zip-top freezer bag that has been cut open on three sides so that it opens like a book. Place a ball in the middle of the tortilla press and flatten it into a 4½-inch (11-cm) disc about ⅛ inch (3 mm) thick. If you don't have a tortilla press, flatten each ball using a flat-bottomed, heavy skillet.

Place 1½ packed tablespoons of the filling in the middle of the disc, leaving a small rim; use the bag to fold the dough over the filling, forming a half-moon. Press the edges together with your fingers to seal well. Transfer the empanada to a prepared baking sheet. Repeat with the rest of the dough and filling, keeping the empanadas covered as you go.

FRY THE EMPANADAS AND SERVE: Fit a large baking sheet with a metal cooling rack; set it aside. In a large skillet with high sides, heat 1 to 1½ inches (2.5 to 4 cm) of oil to 360°F (180°C) or use a deep-fryer according to the manufacturer's directions. Working in batches, carefully slide the empanadas into the oil. Fry them until they are golden, about 4 minutes, turning them over halfway through. If the oil gets too hot as you fry and they're browning too quickly, lower the temperature and let the oil cool slightly before frying any more. Use a slotted spoon to transfer the fried empanadas to the prepared rack to drain. Sprinkle them with salt, let them rest for 1 to 2 minutes, and serve.

NOTE: To freeze after frying, cool the empanadas thoroughly and place them in a single layer on baking sheets. Freeze until solid; transfer them to freezer bags and freeze for up to 4 months. Heat them in a 350°F (175°C) oven until heated through, 12 to 15 minutes.

SUGAR-COATED PORK AND RAISIN TURNOVERS

I cut my teeth on empanadas such as these sweet, meaty pockets. I created this recipe in honor of my beloved Tía María, who made similar pork pies. My rendition has a moist filling, with a slight hint of tomatoes and a pleasant brininess from the olives hidden inside. The sweet spices are reminiscent of the pie's Moorish culinary influences, harking back to the Middle Ages. The crust is lightly coated with sugar, so that every bite is both sweet and savory.

MAKES 24 TO 26 EMPANADAS

MAKE THE FILLING: In a medium skillet, heat 1 tablespoon of the oil over medium-high heat; cook the onions until they are soft, about 2 minutes. Add the garlic and cook until it is fragrant, about 30 seconds. Add the pork and cook while breaking it up with a wooden spoon until it's no longer pink, 2 to 3 minutes. Add the tomatoes, sour orange juice, cinnamon, salt, pepper, cloves, and thyme. Lower the heat to medium; simmer, uncovered, until the liquid has evaporated, about 5 minutes. Remove the filling from the heat; discard the cinnamon. Stir in the raisins, olives, and almonds. Transfer the mixture to a baking sheet, spreading it out evenly; cover and chill it for at least 2 hours or overnight.

ASSEMBLE THE EMPANADAS: After the filling chills, make the dough as directed on page 29 and let it rest, covered with plastic or with a damp towel, for 1 hour at room temperature. Dust a clean surface with flour; roll out the dough to ⅛ inch (3 mm) thick (like for piecrust). Use a 3½-inch (9-cm) round cutter to cut out 24 to 26 rounds, re-rolling the scraps as needed, until all the rounds are cut (see Notes). Keep the rounds covered with damp cloth as you work. Working

Continued ➡

---

1 tablespoon vegetable oil, plus more for frying

1 cup (120 g) finely chopped white onions

2 large cloves garlic, finely minced

½ pound (255 g) ground pork

½ cup (120 ml) canned crushed tomatoes

2 tablespoons sour orange juice (or half lemon juice, half orange juice)

1 (3-inch/7½-cm) stick Mexican cinnamon (*canela*)

1 teaspoon fine sea salt

¼ teaspoon freshly ground black pepper

¼ teaspoon ground cloves

¼ teaspoon dried thyme

¼ cup (40 g) black raisins

¼ cup (30 g) sliced green olives

¼ cup (30 g) slivered almonds, toasted

1 recipe Master Dough (page 29)

Egg wash, made with 1 beaten egg and 2 teaspoons water

⅓ cup (70 g) sugar

with a few pastry rounds at a time, moisten the edges with the egg wash and place 2 heaping teaspoons of the filling in the middle of each round. Fold the top of the dough over the filling to form half-moon shapes. Press the edges together tightly. Use the tines of a fork to seal the edges shut. It will be helpful to press out the air from the middle of the empanadas as you shape them, so that they don't puff up excessively as they fry. Set the empanadas on a baking sheet (keeping them covered with a clean kitchen towel as you work); refrigerate them uncovered for 1 hour.

FRY THE EMPANADAS AND SERVE: Fit a baking sheet with a metal cooling rack; set it aside. Place the sugar in a shallow bowl; set it aside. In a large Dutch oven, heat 2 inches (5 cm) of oil to 360°F (180°C) or use a deep-fryer according to the manufacturer's instructions. Working in batches, carefully slide the empanadas into the oil and fry them until they are golden, about 2 minutes, turning them halfway through to cook both sides. If the oil gets too hot as you fry and they're browning too quickly, lower the temperature and let the oil cool slightly before frying any more. Use a slotted spoon to remove the empanadas from the oil and place them on the rack to drain; let them cool for 1 minute. While they are still warm, roll them in the sugar, coating all sides. Serve them hot or at room temperature.

NOTES: The less you play with this dough, the more tender it will be, so I suggest you try to cut as many rounds as you possibly can from the first roll. Knead the scraps back together for 30 seconds (just until the dough holds together), cover the dough with plastic or a damp towel, and let it rest for 10 minutes before re-rolling. If the dough still shrinks as you roll it, step back, let it rest on the counter, covered, for 10 minutes, and then roll it out again. To get all of the rounds, you'll have to roll the dough very thinly.

These are best eaten fresh. You can shape the empanadas ahead of time and place them uncooked, in a single layer, on a baking sheet; freeze them until solid, then transfer them to freezer bags and keep them frozen for up to 3 months. Fry them without thawing (to prevent splatters) for 2 to 3 minutes, or until golden. Once fried, roll them in sugar.

SUGAR-COATED
PORK AND RAISIN
TURNOVERS

SWEET AND SAVORY
PORK PIES [PAGE 96]

SWEET AND SAVORY PORK PIES

★ PASTELITOS DE CERDO ★ NICARAGUA ★

2 teaspoons vegetable oil, plus more for frying

½ pound (225 g) ground pork

1 cup (120 g) finely chopped white onions

¼ cup (30 g) finely chopped green bell pepper

2 large cloves garlic, minced

½ teaspoon freshly grated nutmeg

½ teaspoon fine sea salt, or to taste

¾ cup (100 g) peeled and finely diced Yukon gold potatoes, boiled until fork tender

¼ cup (40 g) black raisins

1 tablespoons small capers, rinsed

1 large hard-boiled egg (see page 15), peeled and finely chopped

1 recipe Master Dough (page 29)

Egg wash, made with 1 beaten egg and 2 teaspoons water

1 cup (200 g) sugar

Like many classic dishes in Latin America, these meaty individual pies feature sweet and sour flavors known as *agridulce,* clear descendants of recipes that arrived to the New World with the conquerors in the sixteenth century. The distinctive flavor of nutmeg is a quick giveaway. My Nicaraguan sister-in-law, Tey, introduced me to these plump, round empanadas, widely sold in pastry shops and street-side cafés. They're usually large enough to fill a small plate, but are popular finger food too. Roll them in sugar while they're still warm so it will stick to their surface. If you want an alternative to frying, you can bake these (see page 29): you won't be able to roll them in sugar, but they'll still be delectable. Enjoy them with a cup of coffee as a snack, or with a glass of wine before dinner.

MAKES 12 PASTELITOS

MAKE THE FILLING: In a large sauté pan, heat 2 teaspoons of the oil over medium-high heat. Add the pork, breaking it up with a spoon and cooking it until no pink remains, about 2 minutes. Add the onions, pepper, garlic, nutmeg, and salt; continue cooking until the onion is softened, about 2 minutes. Add the potatoes, raisins, and capers and cook for 2 minutes, stirring constantly. Remove the filling from the heat and let it cool for 10 minutes in the pan. Stir in the chopped egg. Transfer the filling to a bowl; cover and chill it for at least 2 hours or overnight.

ASSEMBLE THE PASTELITOS: After the filling chills, make the dough as directed on page 29 and let it rest, covered with plastic or with a damp towel, for 1 hour at room temperature.

Dust a clean surface with flour. Roll out the dough to ⅛ inch (3 mm) thick (like for piecrust). Use a 3¾-inch (9.5-cm) round cutter to cut 24 rounds, re-rolling the scraps as needed, until all the rounds are cut (see Notes). Keep them covered as you work.

Line two baking sheets with parchment paper; set them aside. Working with one disc at a time, brush the edges with the egg wash. Place 2 tablespoons of the filling in the center of the disc. Top with a second disc; press down the edges to form a ½-inch (12-mm) rim. Use your index finger and thumb to roll and pinch sections of the dough along the rim at ½-inch (12-mm) intervals to form a decorative (rustic) edge (see photo on page 95). Transfer the *pastelito* to a prepared baking sheet. Repeat with the remaining dough and fillings, until all the ingredients are used; refrigerate them uncovered for 1 hour (or up to 4 hours).

FRY THE *PASTELITOS* AND SERVE: Fit a large baking sheet with a metal cooling rack; set it aside. In a Dutch oven, heat 3 inches (7.5 cm) of oil to 360°F (180°C) or use a deep-fryer according to the manufacturer's directions. Working in batches, carefully slide the *pastelitos* into the oil. Fry them until they are golden, about 2 minutes, turning them halfway through to cook both sides. If the oil gets too hot as you fry and they're browning too quickly, lower the temperature and let the oil cool slightly before frying any more. Use a slotted spoon to remove them from the oil and place them on the prepared rack to drain; let them cool for 1 minute. While they are still warm, roll them in the sugar, coating all sides. Let them cool for 1 to 2 minutes and roll them a second time in the sugar. Serve the *pastelitos* warm or at room temperature.

> **NOTES:** The less you play with this dough, the more tender it will be, so I suggest you try to cut as many rounds as you possibly can from the first roll. Knead the scraps back together for 30 seconds (just until the dough holds together), cover the dough with plastic or a damp towel, and let it rest for 10 minutes before re-rolling. If the dough still shrinks as you roll it, step back, let it rest on the counter, covered, for 10 minutes, and then roll it out again. To get all of the rounds, you'll have to roll the dough very thinly.
>
> These are best eaten immediately after they're fried. You can freeze them uncooked in a single layer; once solid, transfer them to freezer bags and keep them frozen for up to 3 months. Fry them without thawing (to prevent splatters) for 2 to 3 minutes, or until golden. Once fried, roll them in the sugar.

CLASSIC HAM AND CHEESE POCKETS

+++

★ EMPANADITAS DE JAMÓN Y QUESO ★
★ CUBA, CENTRAL AMERICA, CHILE, ARGENTINA ★

¼ pound (115 g) finely chopped cooked ham

½ cup (60 g) shredded cheddar, mozzarella, Muenster, or other melting cheese

¼ cup (60 ml) mayonnaise

1 tablespoon mustard (your favorite flavor)

1 recipe Flaky Dough (page 34)

Egg wash, made with 1 beaten egg and 2 teaspoons water

These empanadas are the ultimate comfort food! Melted goodness seeps out of these scrumptious pockets filled with a classic combo. Like kids almost everywhere, Latin American children are familiar with this kind of treat, whether it is fashioned out of puff pastry or, as it is in this case, from Flaky Dough (page 34). This wintertime after-school snack that my daughters would come home to almost every day provided them with quick warm sustenance. Then, as I do now, I'd fashion several batches and flash-freeze them, unbaked. They go easily from freezer to oven to plate in no time! C'mon, bake a batch for your kids or get in touch with your inner child—you'll be so happy you did. Just remember that you need to make the dough at least thirty minutes before making these empanadas.

++

MAKES **16** EMPANADAS

MAKE THE FILLING: In a medium bowl, mix together the ham, cheese, mayonnaise, and mustard. Cover and chill for at least 30 minutes (or up to 24 hours).

ASSEMBLE THE EMPANADAS: After the filling chills, make the dough as directed on page 34 and let it rest, covered with plastic, for at least 30 minutes or up to 24 hours in the refrigerator (if the dough is too cold to roll out, let it sit at room temperature for 10 minutes before rolling).

Line two large baking sheets with parchment paper; set them aside. On a well-floured surface and with a well-floured rolling pin, roll out the pastry to about

Continued ➔

⅛ inch (3 mm) thick (like for piecrust). Keep lightly dusting flour on your surface and rolling pin as you roll so that the pastry doesn't tear or stick (see Notes). Using a round 3½-inch (9-cm) cutter, make 32 rounds, rolling and cutting the scraps as needed. Keep them covered as you work. Place a generous 1 tablespoon of filling in the center of half of the pastry rounds. Working with one round at a time, brush the edges with the egg wash and place another dough round over the filling. Use your fingers to seal the empanadas (they will look like ravioli), being careful to press the air out of the dough as your fingers move to the edges. Seal the edges very well with your fingers and then press them together with the tines of a fork; use the tines of the fork to poke vents on top of each empanada. Transfer the empanadas to the baking sheets and chill them uncovered for 20 minutes (or up to 8 hours).

BAKE THE EMPANADAS AND SERVE: Preheat the oven to 400°F (205°C). Brush the tops of the empanadas with the egg wash. Bake the empanadas until they are golden, 12 to 15 minutes (rotate the pans in the oven halfway through baking, back to front and top to bottom, to ensure that all of the empanadas bake evenly). Let them rest for 2 to 3 minutes and serve them warm.

NOTES: This is sticky dough. For easier rolling, roll the pastry on a generously floured surface, flour the top of the pastry, and use a piece of plastic wrap (or parchment paper) directly over the top of the pastry so that the rolling pin doesn't stick. If you need to re-roll the dough, brush excess flour off the scraps with a clean pastry brush and gather up the scraps; wrap them in plastic and chill them for 10 minutes.

To freeze the unbaked empanadas, do not brush the tops with egg wash. Place them in one layer on the prepared baking sheets and freeze them until solid. Transfer them to freezer-safe bags or bins and keep them frozen for up to 4 months. To reheat, brush the tops of the frozen empanadas with the egg wash. Bake them directly from the freezer. Add 3 to 5 minutes to the baking time, or bake until the empanadas are lightly golden.

CHORIZO AND POTATO PIES WITH TOMATILLO SALSA

These spicy and richly flavored *antojitos* (appetizers) are filled with a classic Mexican filling of potatoes and chorizo sausage. Their crusts are crispy and I love how the meaty chorizo melds with the creamy potatoes, creating a great textural juxtaposition. Mexican chorizo is raw pork sausage seasoned with dried chiles and garlic; don't confuse it with the dried sausages from Spain. It's widely available in grocery stores. You should serve the empanadas with refreshing salsas for another contrast of textures. Although I prefer to fry these, you may also cook them on a griddle.

MAKES **14** EMPANADAS

MAKE THE FILLING: Heat the 2 teaspoons of oil in a large, nonstick skillet set over medium-high heat; add the chorizo and cook it until it has rendered its fat, all the while breaking it down with a wooden spoon, 3 to 4 minutes. Add the onions and cook until they are softened, about 3 minutes. Add the potatoes, poblano pepper, salt, and black pepper; cover, lower the heat to medium, and continue cooking until the potatoes are fork tender, 6 to 8 minutes. Remove the filling from the heat and let it cool completely; cover and chill it for at least 2 hours or up to overnight.

ASSEMBLE THE EMPANADAS: After the filling chills, make the dough as directed on page 24 and let it rest, covered with plastic, for 10 minutes at room temperature.

Line a large baking sheet with parchment paper; set it aside. Divide the dough into 14 equal portions (about 2 ounces/55 g each). Roll each portion into a ball and keep them covered with a damp kitchen towel as you work. Line a tortilla press with

Continued ➡

2 teaspoons vegetable oil, plus more for frying (optional)

¾ pound (340 g) Mexican chorizo, casings removed

1 cup (120 g) finely chopped white onions

3 cups (420 g) peeled and finely chopped Yukon gold potatoes

1 roasted poblano pepper (see page 15), peeled and chopped

1 teaspoons fine sea salt, or to taste

¼ teaspoon freshly ground black pepper, or to taste

1 recipe Masa Dough (page 24)

5 ounces (140 g) crumbled queso fresco or feta cheese, to taste

1 recipe Raw Tomatillo Salsa (page 171) or store-bought salsa

a zip-top freezer bag that has been cut open on three sides so that it opens like a book. Place a ball of dough in the middle of the tortilla press and flatten it into a 5½-inch (14-cm) disc about ⅛ inch (3 mm) thick. If you don't have a tortilla press, use a flat-bottomed, heavy skillet to press the dough. Place 2 tablespoons of the filling in the middle of the disc, leaving a small rim. Use the bag to fold the masa over the filling, forming a half-moon. Press the edges together with your fingers to seal. Transfer the empanada to the prepared baking sheet. Repeat with the rest of the dough and filling, keeping the empanadas covered as you go.

TO FRY THE EMPANADAS: Fit a large baking sheet with a metal cooling rack; set it aside. In a large skillet with high sides, heat 1 to 1½ inches (2.5 to 4 cm) of oil to 360°F (180°C) or use a deep-fryer according to the manufacturer's directions. Working in batches, carefully slide the empanadas into the oil. Fry them until golden, 4 to 6 minutes, turning them over halfway through. If the oil gets too hot as you fry and they're browning too quickly, lower the temperature and let the oil cool slightly before frying any more. Use a slotted spoon to transfer the fried empanadas to the prepared rack to drain.

TO GRILL THE EMPANADAS: Heat a griddle to 375°F (190°C) and cook the empanadas until they develop golden flecks on each side, 4 to 5 minutes per side, turning them over every minute so they don't burn. If the griddle is too hot, the exterior of the empanadas will burn before they cook through. If this happens, reduce the heat of your griddle, wait a few minutes, and proceed. Transfer the finished empanadas to the prepared pan, wrapping them in a damp kitchen towel for 5 to 8 minutes in order to allow them to steam and become tender.

TO SERVE THE EMPANADAS: While they are warm, sprinkle the empanadas with the queso fresco or feta and serve them with the salsa.

> **NOTE:** To freeze the cooked empanadas (whether fried or grilled), place them in a single layer on a baking sheet lined with parchment paper; freeze them until solid and then transfer them to freezer bags. They keep frozen for up to 3 months. To reheat them, place them in a 350°F (175°C) oven for 10 to 12 minutes, or until their centers are hot.

★ CHAPTER 4 ★

CHICKEN EMPANADAS

EVEN THOUGH THE MOST FAMOUS EMPANADAS IN LATIN AMERICA ARE FILLED WITH BEEF, THERE ARE MANY EMPANADAS IN WHICH CHICKEN PLAYS THE STARRING ROLE. CHICKEN HAS A NEUTRAL FLAVOR THAT IS EASILY DRESSED WITH SPICES AND CONDIMENTS, AND THEREFORE IT IS PREFERRED FOR FILLINGS THAT FEATURE VELVETY AND SPICY SAUCES.

In this chapter, you'll find ravioli-shaped empanadas from Peru that are filled with creamy mushroom sauce, and you'll find half-moon–shaped empanadas dressed with spicy yellow pepper and pecan sauce. You'll also discover the many ways in which shredded chicken is transformed into a sweet and savory delicacy, such as in the Nicaraguan sugar-coated empanadas called *pastelitos*. If you ever find yourself with any leftover chicken, turn to these recipes for nifty and scrumptious ways to use it. Learn how to expertly poach a chicken (see page 19) so you can make these empanadas often. And if you're looking for new ways to transform everyday rotisserie chicken into comforting and delightful tidbits, this chapter will serve you well.

CREAMY CHICKEN AND MUSHROOM EMPANADAS

★ EMPANADAS DE POLLO Y HONGOS ★ PERU ★

2 tablespoons unsalted butter

1½ cups (115 g) finely chopped white button mushrooms

¼ cup (30 g) finely chopped white onion

2 tablespoons finely chopped leek

1 large clove garlic, minced

2 tablespoons all-purpose flour

½ cup (120 ml) chicken broth

¼ cup (60 ml) white wine

2 cups (280 g) shredded Poached Chicken (page 19)

1 teaspoon fine sea salt

¼ teaspoon freshly ground black pepper

¼ teaspoon freshly ground nutmeg

1 recipe Flaky Dough (page 34) or 32 store-bought empanada discs (*hojaldrada* style)

Egg wash, made with 1 beaten egg and 2 teaspoons water

These large and plump ravioli-shaped empanadas are have a flaky, crispy crust that surrounds creamy chicken stew. In Lima, empanadas like these are sold in cafés, where they're showcased in giant trays behind glass display windows. These are fancy empanadas, fit to serve with a glass of chilled wine. The recipe for the filling—reminiscent of the stuffing found in pot pies—is easily doubled; you can make twice the number of empanadas and freeze one batch, or simply ladle the sumptuous filling over steamed rice. My Flaky Dough (page 34) is perfect for these, but if you want to cut corners, use purchased empanada discs (see Sources, page 172) and look for the *hojaldrada* kind.

MAKES **16** TO **18** EMPANADAS

MAKE THE FILLING: Melt the butter in a large sauté pan with high sides, set over medium-high heat. Add the mushrooms, onion, leek, and garlic, stirring constantly; cook until the onion is soft, about 4 minutes. Stir in the flour and cook for 1 minute, stirring constantly. Add the broth and wine, stirring well; lower the heat to medium and simmer for 1 to 2 minutes, or until a thick sauce has formed. Stir in the chicken, salt, pepper, and nutmeg and heat them through for 1 minute. Remove the filling from the heat; let it cool, cover, and chill it completely before using, at least 2 hours or overnight.

ASSEMBLE THE EMPANADAS: After the filling chills, make the dough as directed on page 34 and let it rest, covered with plastic for at least 30 minutes or up to 24 hours in the refrigerator (if the dough is too cold to roll out, let it sit at room temperature for 10 minutes before rolling).

Line two large baking sheets with parchment paper. On a well-floured surface and with a well-floured rolling pin, roll out the pastry to about ⅛ inch (3 mm) thick (like for piecrust). Keep lightly dusting flour on your surface and rolling pin as you roll so that the pastry doesn't tear or stick (see Notes). Using a 3¼-inch (8.5-cm) round cutter, make 36 rounds or use 3½-inch (9-cm) cutters to make 32 rounds, rolling and cutting the scraps as needed. Keep them covered as you work.

Place a generous 1 tablespoon of filling in the center of half of the pastry rounds. Working with one round at a time, brush the edges with the egg wash and place another dough round over the filling. Use your fingers to seal the edges (the empanadas will look like ravioli), being careful to press the air out of the dough as your fingers move to the edges. After sealing very well with your fingers, press the edges together well with the tines of a fork; use the tines of the fork to poke vents on top of each empanada. Transfer the empanadas to the baking sheets and chill them uncovered for 20 minutes (or up to 8 hours).

BAKE THE EMPANADAS AND SERVE: Preheat the oven to 400°F (205°C). Brush the tops of the empanadas with the egg wash. Bake the empanadas until they are golden, 12 to 15 minutes (rotating the pans back to front, top to bottom, halfway through). Let them rest for 2 to 3 minutes before serving them warm.

NOTES: This is sticky dough. For easier rolling, roll the pastry on a generously floured surface, flour the top of the pastry, and place a piece of plastic wrap (or parchment paper) directly over the top of the pastry so that the rolling pin doesn't stick. If you need to re-roll the dough, brush excess flour off the scraps with a clean pastry brush and gather up the scraps; wrap them in plastic and chill them for 10 minutes.

To freeze the unbaked empanadas, do not brush the tops with egg wash. Place them in one layer on the prepared baking sheets and freeze them until solid. Transfer them to freezer-safe bags or boxes and freeze them for up to 4 months. To reheat, brush the tops of the frozen empanadas with the egg wash. Bake them directly from the freezer in a 350°F (175°C) oven, adding 3 to 5 more minutes to the baking time, or bake until they're golden.

CREAMY CHICKEN
AND MUSHROOM
EMPANADAS [PAGE 106]

CHICKEN MASA PIES WITH LETTUCE AND RADISHES

+++

★ DOBLADAS DE POLLO ★ GUATEMALA ★

2 cups (280 g) shredded Poached Chicken (page 19)

1 cup (185 g) seeded and minced plum tomatoes

⅓ cup (50 g) peeled and minced carrots

1 large serrano pepper, minced (seeded and deveined, if less heat is desired)

1 teaspoon fine sea salt, or to taste

¼ teaspoon freshly ground black pepper, or to taste

1 recipe Masa Dough (page 24)

Vegetable oil for frying

1 recipe Raw Tomatillo Salsa (page 171) or Dried Chile, Bell Pepper, and Tomato Sauce (page 169)

Shredded iceberg lettuce for serving

Thinly sliced radishes for serving

Hot sauce for serving (your favorite brand)

Going to "La Terminal"—the main marketplace in Guatemala City—was always an adventure when I was growing up. I went a few times with my grandmother's cook, Felipa. One of our favorite things to do after she finished shopping for ingredients was to stop by the stand where the *dobladas* were being fried to order. By that time, we had usually worked up an appetite, and I was always eager to eat something crunchy and piping hot. *Doblada* means "folded," and these masa empanadas were usually filled with simple ingredients—a bit of cheese, a touch of herbs, and sometimes meat. There are many ways of shaping empanadas, but when you see a masa pie shaped like a half-moon anywhere in Central America, it is called a *doblada*. The fun began when we made our way to the condiment table—a rustic, wooden plank set over stools—brimming full of salsas and other toppings. Here is my rendition of those *dobladas*, which haunt my memory with images of times past (sadly, the market burnt down to ashes in 2014).

+++

MAKES 12 DOBLADAS

MAKE THE FILLING: In a medium bowl, stir together the chicken, tomatoes, carrots, serrano pepper, salt, and black pepper until combined. Chill the filling, covered, for at least 30 minutes or overnight.

ASSEMBLE THE DOBLADAS: After the filling chills, make the dough as directed on page 24 and let it rest, covered with plastic, for 10 minutes at room temperature.

Line a large baking sheet with parchment paper; set it aside. Divide the dough into 12 equal portions (about 2½ ounces/70 g each). Roll each portion into a ball and

Continued ➡

keep them covered with a damp kitchen towel as you work. Line a tortilla press with a zip-top freezer bag that has been cut open on three sides so that it opens like a book. Place a ball of masa in the middle of the tortilla press and flatten it into a 5½-inch (14-cm) disc about ⅛ inch (3 mm) thick. If you don't have a tortilla press, use a flat-bottomed, heavy skillet to press the dough. Place 2 heaping tablespoons of the filling in the middle of the disc, leaving a small rim. Use the bag to fold the masa over the filling, forming a half-moon. Press the edges together with your fingers to seal. Transfer the *dobladas* to the prepared baking sheet. Repeat with the rest of the dough and filling, keeping the *dobladas* covered as you go.

FRY THE *DOBLADAS* AND SERVE: Fit a large baking sheet with a metal cooling rack; set it aside. In a large skillet with high sides, heat 1 to 1½ inches (2.5 to 4 cm) of oil to 360°F (180°C) or use a deep-fryer according to the manufacturer's directions. Working in batches, carefully slide the *dobladas* into the oil. Fry them until golden, 4 to 6 minutes, turning them over halfway through. If the oil gets too hot as you fry and they're browning too quickly, lower the temperature and let the oil cool slightly before frying any more. Use a slotted spoon to transfer the fried *dobladas* to the prepared rack to drain. Let them rest for 1 to 2 minutes and then serve with the salsa, lettuce, radishes, and hot sauce, or keep them warm for up to 1 hour in a 250°F (120°C) oven before serving.

> **NOTE:** To freeze the fried *dobladas*, place them in a single layer on a baking sheet lined with parchment paper; freeze them until solid and then transfer them to freezer-safe bags or bins. They keep frozen for up to 3 months. Reheat them in a 350°F (175°C) oven for 12 to 15 minutes, or until the filling is hot.

SWEET AND SAVORY CHICKEN, ROASTED RED PEPPER, AND OLIVE PIES

★ PASTELITOS DE POLLO ★ NICARAGUA ★

Puffy dough sparkles with sugar and hugs sweet and savory chicken. *Pastelitos* means "small cakes." My sister-in-law's mom, Esther de Sugrañes, is Nicaraguan; this is a loose adaptation of the empanadas she often purchases near her home. Fry them only when you're ready to serve them and roll them in sugar while they're still warm so that it sticks to their crusts. Worcestershire sauce is a key ingredient in Nicaraguan cuisine, yet it's so hard to pronounce (even for native English speakers!) that Latin Americans simply call it *salsa inglesa* or "English sauce." Roll out the dough thinly or these *pastelitos* will be doughy in the center. If you want an alternative to frying, you can bake these (see page 29); you won't be able to roll them in sugar, but they'll still be delectable.

+ +

MAKES **12** *PASTELITOS*

MAKE THE FILLING: Heat the olive oil in a medium nonstick pan over medium-high heat. Add the onion and roasted pepper and sauté until the onion is softened, about 3 minutes. Add the olives, capers, tomato paste, Worcestershire sauce, mustard, and ½ cup (120 ml) water and stir them together well. Lower the heat to medium-low and cook until the sauce is thickened, about 4 minutes. Stir in the chicken, salt, and black pepper; remove the filling from the heat and let it cool completely. Cover and chill it for at least 3 hours or overnight.

ASSEMBLE THE *PASTELITOS*: After the filling chills, make the dough as directed on page 29 and let it rest, covered with plastic or with a damp towel, for 1 hour at room temperature.

Line two baking sheets with parchment paper; set them aside. Dust a clean surface with flour. Roll out the dough to ⅛ inch (3 mm) thick (like for piecrust). Use a

2 teaspoons extra-virgin olive oil

½ cup (60 g) finely chopped white onion

½ cup (130 g) finely chopped roasted red bell pepper (see page 15)

½ cup (55 g) finely chopped green olives

¼ cup (35g) small capers, drained and roughly chopped

2 tablespoons tomato paste

2 tablespoons Worcestershire sauce

1 tablespoon yellow or brown mustard

2 cups (280 g) finely chopped Poached Chicken (page 19)

¼ teaspoon fine sea salt, or to taste

¼ teaspoon freshly ground black pepper, or to taste

1 recipe Master Dough (page 29)

Egg wash, made with 1 beaten egg and 2 teaspoons water

Vegetable oil for frying

1 cup (200 g) sugar

Continued ➔

3¾-inch (9.5-cm) round cutter to cut 24 rounds, re-rolling the scraps as needed, until all the rounds are cut (see Notes). Keep them covered as you work. Working with one disc at a time, brush the edges with the egg wash. Place 2 tablespoons of the filling in the center of the disc. Top with a second disc; press down the edges to form a ½-inch (12-mm) rim. Use your index finger and thumb to roll and pinch sections of the dough along the rim at ½-inch (12-mm) intervals to form a decorative (rustic) edge. It will be helpful to press out the air from the middle of the *pastelitos* as you shape them, so that they don't puff up excessively as they fry. Transfer the *pastelito* to a prepared baking sheet. Repeat with the remaining dough and filling, until all the ingredients are used; refrigerate them uncovered for 1 hour (or up to 4 hours) before cooking.

FRY THE *PASTELITOS* AND SERVE: Fit a large baking sheet with a metal cooling rack; set it aside. In a Dutch oven, heat 3 inches (7.5 cm) of vegetable oil to 360°F (180°C) or use a deep-fryer according to the manufacturer's directions. Working in batches, carefully slide the *pastelitos* into the oil. Fry them until they are golden, about 2 minutes, turning them halfway through to cook both sides. If the oil gets too hot as you fry and they're browning too quickly, lower the temperature and let the oil cool slightly before frying any more. Use a slotted spoon to remove them from the oil and place them on the prepared rack to drain; let them cool for 1 minute. While they are still warm, roll them in the sugar, coating all sides. Let them cool for 1 to 2 minutes and roll them a second time in the sugar. Serve the *pastelitos* warm or at room temperature.

NOTES: The less you play with this dough, the more tender it will be, so I suggest you try to cut as many rounds as you possibly can from the first roll. Knead the scraps back together for 30 seconds (just until the dough holds together), cover it with plastic or with a damp towel, and let it rest for 10 minutes before re-rolling. If the dough still shrinks as you roll it, step back, let it rest on the counter, covered, for 10 minutes, and then roll it out again. To get all of the rounds, you'll have to roll the dough very thinly.

These are best eaten immediately after frying. You can freeze the uncooked *pastelitos* in a single layer; once solid, transfer them to bags and freeze them for up to 1 month. They can go directly from freezer to fryer without thawing. Fry them for about 3 minutes, or until crispy and golden. Roll them in the sugar and serve.

CHICKEN PIES WITH PECAN AND YELLOW PEPPER SAUCE

+++

★ EMPANADAS DE AJÍ DE GALLINA ★ PERU ★

1 tablespoon olive oil

1 cup (120 g) roughly chopped white onions

2 large cloves garlic, halved

14 saltine crackers, coarsely crumbled between your fingers

1 cup (240 ml) chicken broth

¾ cup (180 ml) evaporated milk

¼ cup (30 g) pecan halves

1 tablespoon *ají amarillo* paste, or to taste

3½ cups (490 g) shredded Poached Chicken (page 19)

1 teaspoon fine sea salt, or to taste

¼ teaspoon freshly ground black pepper, or to taste

1 recipe Bread Dough (page 30)

5 hard-boiled eggs (see page 15), peeled and sliced into sixths

1 (6-ounce/170-g) can pitted black olives, drained

Egg wash, made with 1 beaten egg and 2 teaspoons water

Ají de gallina is a spicy Peruvian stew made with chicken drowned in a velvety sauce of pecans and yellow peppers known as *ajíes amarillos*. The stew is traditionally served over a mound of steamed rice. However, empanadas stuffed with *ají de gallina* have become very trendy in Peru as of late and you'll now find them served in both fancy and casual restaurants all over the city of Lima. You can buy whole *ajíes amarillos* in jars, but they're easier to use when transformed into paste (see Sources, page 172). The sauce is thickened with saltine crackers. Make the stew several hours ahead of time so that it has time to chill and thicken.

+++

MAKES 28 EMPANADAS

MAKE THE FILLING: Heat the olive oil in a medium nonstick skillet over medium-high heat. Add the onions and garlic and cook until the onions begin to soften and turn slightly golden, about 2 minutes. Remove the pan from the heat and set the vegetables aside to cool. Place the cooled mixture in a blender. Add the crackers, broth, evaporated milk, pecans, and *ají* paste. Blend until smooth. Return the sauce to the skillet and set it over medium-high heat, stirring until the sauce thickens, about 4 minutes. Remove it from the heat. Stir the chicken, salt, and black pepper into the sauce and let cool for 20 minutes. Transfer the stew to a large bowl; cover and chill it for at least 6 hours or overnight.

ASSEMBLE THE EMPANADAS: After the filling chills, make the dough as directed on page 30 and let it rest, covered with plastic wrap, for 10 minutes at room temperature.

Continued ➡

Line two baking sheets with parchment paper; set them aside. Divide the dough into 28 equal pieces (about 2 ounces/55 g each). Roll each piece into a ball, folding the bottom of the dough onto itself so that the ends are at the bottom and the tops are smooth (the way you'd shape rolls). Place them on a lightly floured baking sheet and cover them with a clean towel; let them rest for 10 minutes. On a well-floured surface, press each ball slightly into a flat disc. Line a tortilla press with a zip-top freezer bag that has been cut open on three sides so that it opens like a book. Place a disc in the middle of the tortilla press and flatten it into a 6-inch (15-cm) round, about ⅛ inch (3 mm) thick (or roll it out with a rolling pin). Stack the discs with parchment paper in between to avoid sticking.

Place 2 heaping tablespoons of the filling in the center of each disc; add a piece of egg and one or two olives (to taste). Fold the bottom of the dough to meet the top of the disc, encasing the filling and forming a half-moon, and press the edges together well. Make ½-inch (12-mm) edges by pressing the rims between your fingers using the *repulgue* method (see page 31). Place the empanadas on the prepared pans. They can sit uncovered at room temperature for 20 minutes before baking or can be refrigerated for up to 1 hour before baking.

BAKE THE EMPANADAS AND SERVE: Preheat the oven to 400°F (205°C). Brush the empanadas with the egg wash. Bake them for 35 to 40 minutes, or until they're golden (rotate the pans in the oven halfway through baking, back to front and top to bottom, to ensure that all of the empanadas bake evenly). Transfer the empanadas to a cooling rack; let them cool for 10 minutes before serving.

NOTE: To freeze these empanadas, cool them to room temperature; set them in a single layer on a baking sheet and freeze them until solid. Transfer them to zip-top bags or freezer boxes and freeze them for up to 4 months. Reheat them in a 350°F (175°C) oven until warmed through, about 15 minutes.

STEWED CHICKEN AND ANNATTO CORN EMPANADAS

The corn empanadas found in the area of Sucre, Venezuela, are recognizable for their golden color and sweet undertone. The stewed fillings, called *guisos*, are seasoned with a blend of aromatics known as *sofrito*. Sucre's *sofrito* features tomato paste and a pepper known as *ají dulce*. These peppers visually resemble habanero peppers but lack their angry heat. If you can't find them, my friend author Maricel Presilla suggests using the smaller sweet peppers of the Caribbean known as *cachuchas* (see the image on page 13) or a seeded and deveined serrano chile.

MAKES 15 EMPANADAS

MAKE THE FILLING: Heat ¼ cup (60 ml) of the oil and the annatto seeds in a small pot over medium heat until they begin to bubble slightly, about 2 minutes. Remove the pot from the heat; let the seeds steep for 15 minutes. Strain the oil into a bowl; discard the seeds.

In a large skillet, heat 2 tablespoons of the annatto oil over medium-high heat. Add the onions, leeks, *ají* or serrano pepper, garlic, and parsley; cook until the onions have softened, about 4 minutes. Add the tomato paste and stir well for 30 seconds; stir in 1 cup (240 ml) water and cook until the mixture thickens slightly, about 1 minute. Remove from the heat and let cool; add the chicken and stir to combine. Season the filling with the salt and black pepper; cover and chill it for at least 2 hours or overnight.

ASSEMBLE THE EMPANADAS: After the filling chills, make the dough as directed on page 27; add the sugared water and the remaining 2 tablespoons annatto oil, kneading it until the dough is uniformly colored. Cover and let it rest for 10 minutes.

Continued ➜

¼ cup (60 ml) vegetable oil, plus more for frying

2 teaspoons annatto seeds (achiote)

1 cup (120 g) minced white onions

½ cup (50 g) minced leeks (white and light green parts only)

1 *ají dulce* or serrano pepper, seeded, deveined, and minced

1 large clove garlic, minced

2 tablespoons minced fresh parsley (leaves and tender stems)

¼ cup (60 ml) tomato paste

3 cups (420 g) shredded Poached Chicken (page 19)

1 teaspoon fine sea salt, or to taste

½ teaspoon freshly ground black pepper, or to taste

1 recipe Cornmeal Dough (page 26)

1 tablespoon sugar dissolved in 2 tablespoons hot water

Line two baking sheets with parchment paper; set them aside. Divide the dough into 15 equal pieces (about 2½ ounces/70 g each). Line a tortilla press with a zip-top freezer bag that has been cut open on three sides so that it opens like a book. Place a ball of dough in the middle of the tortilla press and flatten it into a 5-inch (12-cm) round, about ⅛ inch (3 mm) thick (see Notes). If you don't have a tortilla press, flatten each ball using a flat-bottomed, heavy skillet. Place 2 heaping tablespoons of the filling in the middle of the disc, leaving a small rim. Use the bag to fold the dough over the filling, forming a half-moon. Press the edges together with your fingers to seal. Transfer the empanada to a prepared baking sheet. Repeat with the rest of the dough and filling, keeping the empanadas covered as you go. These empanadas can be shaped and filled up to 1 hour before frying as long as you keep them covered and chilled until you're ready to fry.

FRY THE EMPANADAS AND SERVE: Fit a large baking sheet with a metal cooling rack and set it aside. In a large skillet with high sides, heat 1 to 1½ inches (2.5 to 4 cm) of oil to 360°F (180°C) or use a deep-fryer according to the manufacturer's directions. Working in batches of 4 or 5 empanadas at a time, carefully slide them into the oil. Fry them until golden, 3 to 4 minutes, turning them over halfway through. If the oil gets too hot as you fry and they're browning too quickly, lower the temperature and let the oil cool slightly before frying any more. Use a slotted spoon to transfer the fried empanadas to the prepared rack to drain. Serve them immediately, or keep them warm in a 250°F (120°C) oven for up to 1 hour before serving.

NOTES: Some cooks prefer to roll the dough into thicker discs, which yield a meatier texture. I like mine rolled somewhat thin because they produce crispier empanadas; to do so, my tortilla press method (see page 22) is particularly essential, but you can experiment with different methods and thicknesses to find your favorite.

Once fried, these empanadas can be frozen for up to 3 months. Freeze them in a single layer on baking sheets lined with parchment paper. When solid, transfer them to containers. Reheat them at 350°F (175°C) for 12 to 15 minutes, or until their centers are hot.

GREEN TOMATILLO CHICKEN STEW EMPANADAS

+++

★ DOBLADAS DE JOCŌN ★ GUATEMALA ★

8 medium tomatillos, husked, rinsed, and dried

3 green onions, roots trimmed

½ green bell pepper, stemmed and seeded

2 cloves garlic, unpeeled

1 jalapeño pepper

1½ cups (60 g) packed fresh cilantro (leaves and tender stems)

2 tablespoons vegetable oil

1 teaspoon fine sea salt

¼ teaspoon freshly ground black pepper, or to taste

2 cups (280 g) shredded Poached Chicken (page 19)

1 recipe Masa Dough (page 24)

1 recipe Raw Tomatillo Salsa (page 171; optional)

1 cup (120 g) grated queso seco (optional)

Roasted vegetables give these low-fat and mouthwatering empanadas a rustic, nutty flavor. In Guatemala, this stew is known as *jocón*, and it's usually served over rice (in fact, you can serve the filling like this). Leftovers are usually reserved for empanadas that are cooked on a griddle rather than fried. The natural pectin in the tomatillos thickens the sauce into a gelatinous substance that makes these a cinch to stuff. As the *dobladas* cook, the sauce melts and becomes unctuous. Fry them if you prefer (see Chicken Masa Pies with Lettuce and Radishes on page 110 for instructions). You can serve them alone or you can top them with my Raw Tomatillo Salsa (page 171) and queso seco. Although they're not traditionally garnished with anything else, you can gild the lily and sprinkle these with shredded lettuce or cabbage, sliced onions, or radishes and make a whole meal out of them.

++

MAKES **12** *DOBLADAS*

MAKE THE FILLING: Set a dry skillet—preferably cast iron—over high heat. Add the tomatillos, onions, and bell pepper; roast while turning them until they're charred all over. Place them in the jar of a blender as they are finished. Add the unpeeled garlic and the jalapeño pepper to the skillet; roast them until charred. Peel the roasted garlic; discard the skin. Stem, seed, and devein the jalapeño. Add them to the blender. Add the cilantro and puree everything until smooth, adding a little water, if necessary, to help the motor run.

Heat the oil in a large pot over medium-high heat. Add the blended vegetables and stir well. You should hear a sizzling sound when the sauce comes into contact with the oil—watch out for sputters. Lower the heat to medium; season the sauce

Continued ➜

with the salt and black pepper and simmer it for 2 minutes. Add the chicken; stir well and simmer until the stew has thickened, 8 to 10 minutes. Remove the filling from the heat; let it cool completely. Transfer it to a bowl; cover and chill it for at least 2 hours or up to overnight.

ASSEMBLE THE *DOBLADAS:* After the filling chills, make the dough as directed on page 24 and let it rest, covered with plastic, for 10 minutes at room temperature.

Line a large baking sheet with parchment paper; set it aside. Divide the dough into 12 equal portions (about 2½ ounces/70 g each). Roll each portion into a ball and keep them covered with a damp kitchen towel as you work. Line a tortilla press with a zip-top freezer bag that has been cut open on three sides so that it opens like a book. Place a ball of masa in the middle of the tortilla press and flatten it into a 5½-inch (14-cm) disc about ⅛ inch (3 mm) thick. If you don't have a tortilla press, use a flat-bottomed, heavy skillet to press the dough. Place 2 heaping tablespoons of the filling in the middle of the disc, leaving a small rim. Use the bag to fold the masa over the filling, forming a half-moon. Press the edges together with your fingers to seal. Transfer the *dobladas* to the prepared baking sheet. Repeat with the rest of the dough and filling, keeping the *dobladas* covered as you go. After filling, cover and chill the shaped *dobladas* for up to 1 hour before cooking.

GRILL THE *DOBLADAS* AND SERVE: Heat a griddle to 375°F (190°C) and cook the *dobladas* until they develop golden flecks on each side, 4 to 5 minutes per side, turning them over every minute so they don't burn. If the griddle is too hot, the exterior of the *dobladas* will burn before they cook through. If this happens, reduce the heat of your griddle, wait a few minutes, and proceed. Transfer the finished *dobladas* to the baking sheet, wrapping them in a damp kitchen towel for 5 to 8 minutes in order to allow them to steam and become tender. Serve them with the Raw Tomatillo Salsa and queso seco, if desired.

NOTE: These don't freeze well, but you can refrigerate the cooked *dobladas* for up to 1 day. Reheat them at 350°F (175°C) for 10 to 12 minutes, or until their centers are hot.

GOLDEN CHICKEN, POTATO, AND GREEN PEA PIES

★ SALTEÑAS DE POLLO ★ BOLIVIA ★

Cut into one of these football-shaped chicken pies, and enjoy a sweet crust and savory filling: Bright yellow crusts with brown edges hide a moist stew inside. The stew is held together with gelatin, which makes it easier to stuff in the dough when it's cold. The discs will shrink a bit as they sit; flatten them out with your hands (or use a rolling pin) before filling the *salteñas*. The dough itself is elastic and will stretch generously over the filling to encase it. Chill the *salteñas* for at least 20 minutes (but better if longer) after you fill them, before baking. These must be very cold or the filling will seep out as it bakes. Serve them with your favorite hot sauce.

++

MAKES 26 TO 28 *SALTEÑAS*

MAKE THE FILLING: In a large, heat-resistant glass bowl, combine the gelatin and broth; stir to mix it together and let it sit for 2 minutes. Heat the gelatin mixture in the microwave on high for 1½ minutes, until the gelatin is dissolved (or over medium-low heat in a double boiler for 3 to 4 minutes); set aside.

Heat the oil in a large skillet over medium-high heat. Add the onions and bell peppers; cook until they are softened, 3 to 4 minutes. Add the paprika and annatto or Bijol; cook for 30 seconds. Add the broth mixture, stirring until the spices are dissolved. Add the potatoes, chicken, peas, parsley, sugar, salt, cumin, oregano, and black pepper; bring the liquid to a boil and cook, uncovered, until the potatoes are tender, about 6 minutes. Transfer the stew to a medium bowl and set it over a large bowl of iced water to cool it quickly. Cool the stew completely; cover it with plastic wrap and chill it for at least 6 hours or overnight (the mixture will jell).

Continued ➜

1 tablespoon unflavored gelatin

2½ cups (600 ml) cold chicken broth

2 tablespoons vegetable oil

1 cup (120 g) finely chopped white onions

1 cup (100 g) finely chopped green bell peppers

1 tablespoon sweet smoked Spanish paprika (pimentón)

1 tablespoon annatto paste (achiote) or Bijol (see Notes on page 40)

2 cups (280 g) peeled and finely chopped Yukon gold potatoes

2 cups (280 g) packed shredded Poached Chicken (page 19)

1 cup (120 g) green peas

½ cup (20 g) finely chopped fresh parsley (tender stems and leaves)

1 tablespoon sugar

1½ teaspoons fine sea salt

1½ teaspoons ground cumin

1 teaspoon dried oregano

¼ teaspoon freshly ground black pepper

1 recipe *Salteña* Dough (page 32)

Egg wash, made with 1 beaten egg and 2 teaspoons water

ASSEMBLE THE *SALTEÑAS*: After the filling chills, make the dough as directed on page 32 and let it rest, covered with plastic or with a damp towel, for 45 to 60 minutes at room temperature. Dust two baking sheets with flour; set them aside. Divide the dough into 26 to 28 equal portions (about 3 ounces/85 g each). Roll each piece into a ball, folding the bottom of the dough onto itself so that the ends are at the bottom and the tops are smooth (the way you'd shape rolls). Place them on the prepared baking sheets and cover them with a clean towel; let them rest for 20 minutes.

Line two baking sheets with parchment paper; set them aside. Working one at a time on a lightly floured surface, flatten each ball slightly into a disc. Line a tortilla press with a zip-top freezer bag that has been cut open on three sides so that it opens like a book. Place the disc in the middle of the tortilla press and press the dough into a 6-inch (15-cm) disc, about 1/8 inch (3 mm) thick (or roll it out with a rolling pin). Stack the discs with parchment paper in between to avoid sticking. Place 3 heaping tablespoons of the jelled filling in the middle of the disc; bring the edges of the pastry together, letting the dough stretch over the filling. Enclose the filling (press the filling down with your forefinger to compact it). Form a half-moon and, holding it by the top edges, stand the *salteña* on its bottom, flattening it so it can stand without toppling. Pinch the edges tightly, and press to form a small rim, about 1/2 inch (12 mm) wide. Then pinch and fold sections of the rim decoratively to seal it well (as you would a dumpling, by gathering the dough starting at one end and pressing it together at 1/2-inch/12-mm intervals, until it's all sealed). Stand the *salteñas* on the prepared pans and chill them for at least 20 minutes (or up to 2 hours). Do not crowd the *salteñas* together in the baking sheet, or their sides will stick and the juices will ooze out.

BAKE THE *SALTEÑAS* AND SERVE: Preheat the oven to 425°F (220°C). Brush the *salteñas* with the egg wash. Bake them for 35 to 40 minutes, or until they are golden (rotate the pans in the oven halfway through baking, back to front and top to bottom, to ensure that all of the *salteñas* bake evenly). Transfer the *salteñas* to a cooling rack. Let them cool for 5 to 10 minutes before serving.

NOTE: Freeze the *salteñas* in a single layer after baking. When solid, transfer to containers and freeze for up to 4 months; reheat them in a 350°F (175°C) oven until hot, 15 to 20 minutes.

CHAPTER 5

★ ★

FISH &
SEAFOOD
EMPANADAS

WHEN SPANISH CONQUERORS BEGAN SETTLING IN THE NEW WORLD IN THE EARLY SIXTEENTH CENTURY, THEY BROUGHT MANY CULINARY TRADITIONS WITH THEM. AMONG THOSE CUSTOMS WAS A STRONG RELIGIOUS BELIEF THAT ENFORCED EATING FISH AND SEAFOOD DURING THE LENTEN SEASON. AMONG THE FIRST EMPANADAS THAT WERE ABSORBED BY THE LATIN CULTURE WERE THOSE MADE WITH FISH IN THE STYLE OF GALICIA, SPAIN. All the way from Mexico to Argentina, and regardless of what the religious beliefs of Latin Americans are today, it is still customary to find an abundance of fish and seafood empanadas made during the weeks preceding Easter. The recipes I selected for this chapter feature ingredients that are pretty standard throughout Latin America. I always keep canned tuna in my pantry and frozen shrimp (or langoustines) in my freezer that can easily be used to make these hand-held pies. Some ingredients, like dried cod, cannot be found in every supermarket; however, you'll find it easily in both Latin and Asian stores, particularly during the spring and at Christmastime, when it is most customary to eat it. Buy it in bulk, as it lasts a very long time, and use it to make the empanadas I feature here, filled with potatoes and a deliciously briny tomato sauce. In this chapter, you'll also find delicately flavored seafood empanadas such as the Argentinean langoustine pies. They're so elegant that you'll want to serve them with sparkling wine. And you'll find rustic tuna empanadas from a small town in Mexico that are best served alongside a cold beer, with plenty of lime wedges. Select a different kind of empanada to eat every Friday night during Lent each year. Or enjoy them just for the sake of eating great seafood pies!

SHRIMP AND TOMATO STEW FLAKY PILLOWS

★ PASTÉIS DE CAMARÃO ★ BRAZIL ★

2 teaspoons extra-virgin olive oil

1 cup (120 g) finely chopped white onions

⅔ cup (120 g) peeled, seeded, and chopped plum tomatoes

2 tablespoons tomato paste

¼ cup (10 g) chopped fresh cilantro (leaves and tender stems)

1 teaspoon fine sea salt, or to taste

12 ounces (340 g) peeled and cooked shrimp or langoustines, cut into ½-inch (12-mm) pieces

1 recipe *Pastéis* Dough (page 33) (or 12 store-bought annatto-flavored empanada discs)

Vegetable oil for frying

These empanadas are plump with shrimp—juicy and messy to eat. In Brazil, they're called *pastéis de camarão*. The shrimp are coated with a sauce called *molho* or "wet sauce," rich in tomato goodness. In Bahia, they're served wrapped in paper to catch the juices. I make several batches ahead of time and freeze them, uncooked, so that I can fry them whenever the craving hits me. Paired with a green salad and a glass of wine, they make a delicious and easy supper in no time. If you don't want to go through the trouble of making your own dough, use packaged annatto-flavored empanada discs for frying (as pictured, opposite), or large egg roll wrappers. Shape them into half-moons or rolls (respectively), instead of making rectangles. If you're lucky enough to find crawfish or langoustines, use them in place of shrimp.

++

MAKES **12** *PASTÉIS*

MAKE THE FILLING: Heat the olive oil in a large skillet set over medium-high heat. Add the onions and sauté until they are golden, about 2 minutes. Add the tomatoes and tomato paste; sauté for 1 minute. Add ¼ cup (60 ml) water and stir well to form a thick paste. Add the cilantro and salt; remove from the heat and let cool slightly. Add the shrimp or langoustines and stir well. Transfer the filling to a large bowl; cover and chill it for at least 30 minutes or up to overnight.

ASSEMBLE THE *PASTÉIS*: While the filling chills, make the dough as directed on page 33 and let it rest, covered with plastic, for 20 minutes at room temperature.

Continued ➜

Line a large baking sheet with parchment paper; set it aside. Divide the dough in half. Roll out the first half to 1/16 inch (2 mm) thick (like for pasta). Using a pastry cutter or very sharp knife, cut it into 5-by-6-inch (12-by-15-cm) rectangles. Re-roll the scraps together, wrap them in the plastic, and allow them to rest for 20 minutes. In the meantime, repeat with the other half of the dough, cutting and re-rolling the scraps (while allowing the dough to rest in between) until you have 12 rectangles. You may have to do this a third time, until all are cut. The bottom side of the rectangles will be sticky; the top should be dry.

With a shorter side toward you and the sticky side facing up, place 2 tablespoons of the filling in the bottom half of each rectangle, leaving 1/2 inch (12 mm) all around. Fold the top over the filling and seal all of the sides well by pressing them together with your fingers. Crimp them tightly with the tines of a fork. Transfer them to the prepared baking sheet.

FRY THE *PASTÉIS* AND SERVE: Fit a large baking sheet with a metal cooling rack; set it aside. In a large skillet with high sides, heat 1/2 to 1 inch (about 2 cm) of vegetable oil to 360°F (180°C) or use a deep-fryer according to the manufacturer's directions. Working in batches, carefully slide the *pastéis* into the oil. Fry them until they're puffy and golden, 1½ to 2 minutes, turning them over halfway through. If the oil gets too hot as you fry and they're browning too quickly, lower the temperature and let the oil cool slightly before frying any more. Remove them with a slotted spoon and place them on the prepared rack to drain. Let them cool for 1 to 2 minutes and serve.

NOTE: *Pastéis* are best fried immediately after shaping and eaten immediately after they're fried. Freeze them uncooked in a single layer; once solid, transfer them to freezer bags and keep them frozen for up to 3 months. Fry them without thawing (to prevent splatters) for 3 to 3½ minutes, or until they are golden and crispy.

CREAMY TUNA AND ROASTED RED PEPPER PIES

Thick béchamel sauce creates a velvety texture that bakes beautifully when wrapped in pastry, resulting in a creamy filling that is subtle and elegant. This may be a very inexpensive recipe to re-create, but these empanadas taste luxurious and appeal to most palates. If you like tuna melts, you'll like these. My children loved to find them hidden in their lunchboxes when they were little. I love the versatility of frozen, store-bought empanada discs and keep a stack of them in my freezer at all times so that I can make these. The fact that the filling is dense makes it easy to stuff into the prepared discs. Look for the words *para hornear* or *hojaldradas* on the package, so you can bake with them. If you prefer to fry them, use regular empanada discs or egg roll wrappers. If you prefer to make your own dough, use the Masa Dough (page 24) and fry the empanadas, or use the Bread Dough (page 30) for baked empanadas. You may substitute jarred roasted peppers, but make sure to pat them dry thoroughly or they'll make the filling watery. Pressing the tuna against a fine sieve is also helpful. In Argentina, some cooks add chopped olives and pieces of hard-boiled eggs.

+++

MAKES **30** EMPANADAS

MAKE THE FILLING: In a medium saucepan set over medium-low heat, melt the butter; add the yellow onions and cook for 3 to 4 minutes, or until they are soft. Add the flour and whisk well; cook it for 1 to 2 minutes, being careful not to let it take any color (it should be shiny and pull away from the sides of the pot). Remove the pot from the heat and add the milk, whisking well until it's the consistency of thick mashed potatoes. Return the pot to the heat and continue cooking

Continued ➤

6 tablespoons (85 g) unsalted butter

1 cup (120 g) minced yellow onions

⅔ cup (85 g) all-purpose flour

1 cup (240 ml) whole milk

¾ teaspoon fine sea salt

¼ teaspoon freshly grated nutmeg

⅛ teaspoon freshly ground white pepper

1 (12-ounce/340-g) can solid white albacore tuna, well drained

2 roasted red bell peppers (see page 15), peeled and finely chopped

½ cup (60 g) grated Parmigiano-Reggiano or Parmesan cheese

3 tablespoons sliced green onions (white and light green parts only)

30 store-bought empanada discs (*hojaldrada* style)

Egg wash, made with 1 beaten egg and 2 teaspoons water

for 2 minutes, constantly stirring and being careful not to burn the sauce. Remove the sauce from the heat; stir in the salt, nutmeg, and white pepper. Transfer the béchamel to a bowl and let it cool for 10 minutes. Add the tuna, roasted peppers, cheese, and green onions, stirring to combine them. Transfer the filling to a large bowl; cover and chill it for at least 2 hours or overnight.

ASSEMBLE THE EMPANADAS: Thaw the empanada discs according to the package directions.

Line two or three large baking sheets with parchment paper; set them aside. Roll the empanada discs with a rolling pin to make them slightly thinner (as per package instructions). Place 2 generous tablespoons of the filling in the bottom half of each disc, leaving a ¼-inch (6-mm) rim. Fold the dough over the filling to form a half-moon. With a fork, press the edges together, crimping them tightly; use the tines of the fork to poke vents on top of each empanada. Transfer the empanadas to the prepared baking sheets. Chill them uncovered for 20 minutes or up to 8 hours.

BAKE THE EMPANADAS AND SERVE: Preheat the oven to 400°F (205°C). Bake the empanadas until they are lightly golden on top, 25 to 30 minutes (rotating the pans back to front, top to bottom, halfway through). Let them rest for 5 minutes before serving them warm.

NOTE: Freeze the baked and cooled empanadas in a single layer on a baking sheet; once solid, transfer them to freezer-safe bags and store them for up to 4 months. Reheat the empanadas in a 350°F (175°C) oven directly from the freezer until the centers are hot, 12 to 15 minutes.

MARIA JOSÉ'S TUNA, JALAPEÑO, AND TOMATO TURNOVERS

++

★ EMPANADAS DE ATÚN ★ MEXICO ★

1 (12-ounce/340-g) can tuna packed in water, drained very well

⅓ cup (60 g) seeded and minced plum tomatoes

¼ cup (30 g) minced red onion

¼ cup (20 g) thinly sliced jalapeño peppers (seeded and deveined for less heat)

¼ cup (10 g) chopped fresh cilantro (leaves and tender stems)

1 teaspoon fine sea salt, or to taste

1 recipe Masa Dough (page 24)

Vegetable oil for frying

3 cups (255 g) finely shredded cabbage or iceberg lettuce

1½ cups (360 ml) Mexican crema or crème fraîche

Lime wedges for serving

1 recipe Raw Tomatillo Salsa (page 171) or Dried Chile, Bell Pepper, and Tomato Sauce (page 169) for serving

Here is another scrumptious empanada filled with tuna. This one has crispy and savory dough hiding a mixture of spicy fish. I got the idea for this recipe from a sweet housekeeper at a hotel where I once stayed during one of my book tours. Her name was Maria José, and she told me of these empanadas popular in the city of Monclova, in the northern state of Coahuila, Mexico. Her mother used to make them and sell them at the market. They are mostly made at home (as opposed to restaurants). Tuna canned in oil is traditional, but I prefer the water-packed fish that is not so greasy. This filling is succulent and studded with chiles, which impart a nice level of heat.

++

MAKES 12 EMPANADAS

MAKE THE FILLING: In a medium bowl, combine the tuna, tomatoes, onion, jalapeños, cilantro, and salt; stir well. Cover and chill the filling for 20 minutes or overnight.

ASSEMBLE THE EMPANADAS: After the filling chills, make the dough as directed on page 24 and let it rest, covered with plastic, for 10 minutes at room temperature.

Line a baking sheet with parchment paper; set it aside. Divide the masa into 12 equal portions (about 2½ ounces/70 g each). Roll each portion into a ball and keep them covered with a damp kitchen towel as you work. Line a tortilla press with a zip-top freezer bag that has been cut open on three sides so that it opens like a book. Place a ball of masa in the middle of the tortilla press and flatten it into

Continued ➜

a 5½-inch (14-cm) disc about ⅛ inch (3 mm) thick. If you don't have a tortilla press, use a flat-bottomed, heavy skillet to press the dough. Place ¼ cup (60 ml) of the filling in the middle of the disc, leaving a small rim. Use the bag to fold the masa over the filling, forming a half-moon. Press the edges together with your fingers to seal. Transfer the empanada to the prepared baking sheet. Repeat with the rest of the dough and filling, keeping the empanadas covered as you go.

FRY THE EMPANADAS AND SERVE: Fit a large baking sheet with a metal cooling rack; set it aside. In a large skillet with high sides, heat 1 to 1½ inches (2.5 to 3 cm) of oil to 360°F (180°C) or use a deep-fryer according to the manufacturer's directions. Working in batches, carefully slide the empanadas into the oil. Fry them until golden, 4 to 6 minutes, turning them over halfway through. If the oil gets too hot as you fry and they're browning too quickly, lower the temperature and let the oil cool slightly before frying any more. Use a slotted spoon to transfer the fried empanadas to the prepared rack to drain. Serve them immediately with the shredded cabbage or lettuce, crema or crème fraîche, lime wedges, and sauce.

NOTE: Freeze the fried empanadas in a single layer on a baking sheet lined with parchment paper; when solid, transfer them to freezer-safe bags or bins. They keep frozen for up to 3 months. Reheat them in a 350°F (175°C) oven for 12 to 15 minutes, or until the filling is hot.

COD AND POTATO TURNOVERS WITH STEWED TOMATOES AND OLIVES

★ EMPANADAS DE CUARESMA ★ VARIOUS COUNTRIES ★

These empanadas are filled with flaky fish bathed in luxurious tomato sauce. Cod made in the style of Viscaya (the Basque region of Spain) is known as *bacalao a la vizcaína*. Dried salted cod is widely available during the Lenten season in any store that caters to Latinos, and in many Asian markets. Once soaked in several changes of water, the fish loses its saltiness and regains its springy texture. My grandmother Mita taught me to soak cod briefly in milk in order to sweeten its flesh even further, but that's optional. Begin soaking the cod at least two days before you intend to make the empanadas; it must be refrigerated during the entire soaking period.

+++

MAKES 26 EMPANADAS

MAKE THE FILLING: Place the cod in a large glass dish and cover it with cold water; cover the dish and refrigerate it. Change the water at least four times in 24 hours. Drain the cod; discard the water and pat the cod dry. (Note: If using milk, soak the cod in the milk in the refrigerator for 2 more hours after the water soak. Drain; discard the milk and pat the cod dry before proceeding.)

With a sharp knife, mince the cod finely; set it aside. In a large nonreactive Dutch oven, heat the oil over medium-high heat. Add the onions and cook until they are softened, 1½ to 2 minutes. Add the garlic and cook until it is fragrant, about 20 seconds; stir in the tomato paste and cook for 30 seconds. Add the tomatoes, roasted peppers, and thyme; stir until combined. Stir in the cod and bring to a simmer; lower the heat, cover, and cook the filling undisturbed for 20 minutes. Stir in the potatoes, olives, and capers. Increase the heat to medium and bring back to a simmer; cover, lower the heat, and simmer the filling until the potatoes are tender, about 15 minutes. Uncover and increase the heat to medium-high. Cook, stirring constantly, until the liquid has

Continued ➡

½ pound (225 g) dried boneless salted cod or pollock (see Sources, page 172)

2 cups (480 ml) whole milk (optional)

3 tablespoons extra-virgin olive oil

1 cup (120 g) finely chopped white onions

6 large cloves garlic, finely minced

2 tablespoons tomato paste

1 (14½-ounce/480-g) can diced tomatoes with juices

2 roasted red bell peppers (see page 15), peeled and finely chopped

½ teaspoon dried thyme

1½ cups (210 g) peeled and finely chopped Yukon gold potatoes

½ cup (55 g) sliced Manzanilla olives

¼ cup (35 g) small capers, drained and rinsed

1 teaspoon fine sea salt, or to taste

½ teaspoon freshly ground black pepper

1 recipe Bread Dough (page 30) or 26 store-bought empanada discs (*hojaldrada* style)

evaporated, about 7 minutes (be careful not to burn the filling). Season with the salt and black pepper (use more or less salt depending on how salty the cod is). Remove the filling from the heat. Transfer it to a medium bowl and set it over a large bowl of iced water to cool it quickly. Cover and chill the filling for at least 4 hours or overnight.

ASSEMBLE THE EMPANADAS: After the filling chills, make the dough as directed on page 30 and let it rest, covered with plastic wrap, for 10 minutes at room temperature.

Line three large baking sheets with parchment paper. Divide the dough into 26 equal pieces (about 2 ounces/55 g each). Roll each piece into a ball, folding the bottom of the dough onto itself so that the ends are at the bottom and the tops are smooth (the way you'd shape rolls). Place them on a lightly floured baking sheet and cover them with a clean towel; let them rest for 10 minutes. Working one at a time, press each ball slightly into a flat disc. Line a tortilla press with a zip-top freezer bag that has been cut open on three sides so that it opens like a book. Place a ball of dough in the middle of the tortilla press and flatten it into a 5-inch (12-cm) round, about ⅛ inch (3 mm) thick (or roll it out with a rolling pin). Stack the discs with parchment paper in between to avoid sticking.

Working with one disc at a time, place 2 tablespoons of the filling in the bottom half of the disc. Fold the bottom of the dough to meet the top of the disc, encasing the filling and forming a half-moon, and press the edges together well. Make ½-inch (12-mm) edges by pressing the rims between your fingers using the *repulgue* method (see page 31). Place the empanadas on the prepared baking sheets. The empanadas can sit uncovered at room temperature for 20 minutes before baking or can be refrigerated for up to 1 hour before baking.

BAKE THE EMPANADAS AND SERVE: Preheat the oven to 425°F (220°C). Bake the empanadas for 25 to 30 minutes, or until they're golden (rotate the pans in the oven halfway through baking, back to front and top to bottom, to ensure that all of the empanadas bake evenly). Transfer the empanadas to a cooling rack; let them rest for 2 to 3 minutes before serving.

> **NOTE:** Freeze the baked and cooled empanadas in a single layer on a baking sheet; once solid, transfer them to freezer-safe bags and store them for up to 4 months. Reheat them in a 350°F (175°C) oven until the centers are hot, 12 to 15 minutes.

★ CHAPTER 6 ★

DESSERT EMPANADAS

SWEET EMPANADAS ABOUND IN LATIN AMERICA. I'VE PUT TOGETHER A COLLECTION OF THOSE RECIPES THAT I BELIEVE ARE MUST-HAVES FOR THE SERIOUS EMPANADA BAKER. IF YOU CAN PUT IT IN A PIE, YOU CAN STUFF IT INTO AN EMPANADA, SO THE NUMBER OF POSSIBLE SWEET HAND-HELD PIES IS TRULY LIMITED ONLY BY THE IMAGINATION. However, every Latin American connoisseur has savored at least one version of fruit and dulce de leche empanadas, such as those found here. Fruit jams and jellies are frequent empanada fillings, and my formula will work with your favorite flavors. There are many fruits that are not available outside of their native countries, such as the *chiverre* (a fruit similar in texture to spaghetti squash that is candied in Costa Rica), or the *jocotes* (tree-tomatoes from Central America) that are frequently made into jams used to fill empanadas. Nor will you be able to find the *ayote* (a gourd with a texture similar to squash but with a yamlike taste) that's caramelized and used to stuff empanadas. Therefore, I've narrowed these recipes to those with ingredients that you will be able to find nearby or online (see Sources, page 172). Make these empanadas as big or as small as you want them to be. Then all you'll need is a good cup of Latin American coffee, yerba mate, or hot chocolate and some time to indulge leisurely in the pleasure of savoring each sweet bite of a hand-held pie.

CARAMEL-APPLE PIES

✦✦✦

★ EMPANADAS DE MANZANA Y DULCE DE LECHE ★
★ ARGENTINA, URUGUAY, CHILE ★

2 large Granny Smith apples, peeled and finely diced

1 tablespoon fresh lemon juice

2 tablespoons unsalted butter

¾ cup (180 ml) thick dulce de leche

2 egg yolks

1 recipe Flaky Dough (page 34)

Egg wash, made with 1 beaten egg and 2 teaspoons water

Confectioners' sugar for dusting

The combination of apples and caramel is a classic. These miniature pies blend a sweet and tart filling with a flaky crust. Dulce de leche is the gooey cow's milk caramel of South America. Purchase the thickest dulce de leche you can find, canned or in jars. If you can't find it at all, substitute it with Mexican *cajeta*, which is a goat's milk caramel, or with any rich caramel sauce. Adding egg yolks to the dulce de leche creates a custardlike texture that stays in place inside the empanadas while they bake. Eat them on their own or with a scoop of good-quality vanilla ice cream.

✦✦✦

MAKES 22 EMPANADAS

MAKE THE FILLING: In a medium bowl, stir the apples together with the lemon juice in order to prevent them from turning brown. Melt the butter in a medium nonstick pan over medium-high heat. Drain the apples to remove any excess juice and add them to the pan. Cook, while stirring, for 3 to 4 minutes, or until they begin to soften but still retain their texture. Remove the apples promptly from the heat and spread them out on a large plate; let them cool completely and chill them for 30 minutes or overnight.

In a medium bowl, stir together the dulce de leche and egg yolks until combined; cover and chill until you're ready to use it.

ASSEMBLE THE EMPANADAS: After the filling chills, make the dough as directed on page 34 and let it rest, covered with plastic, for at least 30 minutes or up to 48 hours in the refrigerator.

Line two large baking sheets with parchment paper. On a well-floured surface and with a well-floured rolling pin, roll out the pastry to about ⅛ inch (3 mm) thick (like for piecrust). Keep lightly dusting flour on your surface and rolling pin as you roll so that the pastry doesn't tear or stick (see Notes). Using a 4-inch (10-cm) round cutter, make 22 rounds, rolling and cutting the scraps as needed.

Working with one disc at a time, place 2 teaspoons of the apple filling on the bottom half of the round and top it with 2 teaspoons of the dulce de leche mixture. Brush the edges of the round with the egg wash and fold it in half over the filling to form a half-moon. Seal the edges of the empanada very well with your fingers and crimp them shut tight with the tines of a fork. It's important to seal these empanadas very well, or you'll have leakage. Use the tines of the fork to poke vents on top of each empanada (flour the fork, if it's sticking). Transfer the empanada to a prepared baking sheet. Repeat with the remaining dough and filling, until all the ingredients are used (discard any leftover dulce de leche mixture at the end). Chill the empanadas uncovered for 20 minutes (or up to 8 hours).

BAKE THE EMPANADAS AND SERVE: Preheat the oven to 400°F (205°C). Brush the tops of the empanadas with the egg wash. Bake until they are golden, 20 to 22 minutes (rotate the pans in the oven halfway through baking, back to front and top to bottom, to ensure that all of the empanadas bake evenly). Transfer the empanadas to cooling racks. When they're slightly cool, sift confectioners' sugar over the tops. Serve them warm or at room temperature.

NOTES: This is sticky dough. For easier rolling, roll the pastry on a generously floured surface, flour the top of the pastry, and use a piece of plastic wrap (or parchment paper) directly over the top of the pastry so that the rolling pin doesn't stick. If you need to re-roll the dough, brush excess flour off the scraps with a clean pastry brush, and gather up the scraps; wrap them in plastic and chill them for 10 minutes.

To freeze the unbaked empanadas, do not brush the tops with egg wash. Place them in one layer on the prepared baking sheets and freeze until solid. Transfer them to freezer-safe containers and keep them frozen for up to 4 months. To reheat, brush the tops of the frozen empanadas with the egg wash. Bake them directly from the freezer, adding 2 to 3 more minutes to the baking time. After they're cooked, dust them with sugar.

CARAMEL-APPLE
PIES [PAGE 144]

CANDIED PINEAPPLE PIES

+++

★ EMPANADAS DE DULCE DE PIÑA ★ COSTA RICA ★

1 ripe pineapple, peeled, cored, and minced

2 cups (400 g) sugar

Grated zest of 1 lemon

Juice of 1 lemon

1 recipe Flaky Dough (page 34)

Egg wash, made with 1 beaten egg and 2 teaspoons water

From Mexico all the way down to Costa Rica, you will find many empanadas filled with sweet, gooey pineapple. I confess to having had my share of them, from the Mexican empanadas filled with fresh pineapple, cinnamon, and raisins, to those found in Costa Rica, made with pineapple jam. Since I'm a huge fan of candied pineapple (known as *piña cristalizada* or *dulce de piña*), I created this rendition. The pineapple must be finely minced, but not to the point where it becomes pulp (you should be able to see small pieces of fruit). This will help it withstand the long cooking time without entirely losing its texture. You will know the candy is ready when you can dip a spoon into it, let it cool for a few seconds, and the mixture jells on the spoon. When refrigerated, the candy will solidify. I suggest you let it sit at room temperature for about an hour before using it so that it's easier to handle. Serve these empanadas (and any leftover pineapple) as part of a cheese course. Any extra candy can be softened to the consistency of jam by simply reheating it over low heat and adding water as needed. Use the sauce to top vanilla ice cream or stir it into a bowl of steamy oatmeal.

+++

MAKES **32** EMPANADAS

MAKE THE FILLING: Place the pineapple and 1 cup (240 ml) water in a medium, nonreactive pot. Bring to a boil over medium-high heat. Lower the heat to medium-low as soon as it reaches a boil; simmer, uncovered, until the pineapple has softened, about 20 minutes. Add the sugar, lemon zest, and lemon juice; stir to combine them. Continue cooking for 50 to 60 minutes, or until the mixture is thickened. Cool the candy slightly and transfer it to a glass container; let it cool completely before using. You can store the candy, covered with plastic wrap or a lid, in the refrigerator for up to 2 weeks.

ASSEMBLE THE EMPANADAS: After the filling chills, make the dough as directed on page 34 and let it rest, covered with plastic, for at least 30 minutes or up to 48 hours in the refrigerator.

Continued ➜

Line two large baking sheets with parchment paper. On a well-floured surface and with a well-floured rolling pin, roll out the pastry to about ⅛ inch (3 mm) thick (like for piecrust). Keep lightly dusting flour on your surface and rolling pin as you roll so that the pastry doesn't tear or stick (see Notes). Using a 3½-inch (9-cm) round cutter, make 32 rounds, rolling and cutting the scraps as needed.

Place 1½ teaspoons of the candied pineapple on the bottom half of each pastry round. Brush the edges of the rounds with the egg wash and fold them in half over the filling to form half-moons. Seal the edges of the empanadas very well with your fingers and crimp them shut tight with the tines of a fork. It's important to seal these empanadas very well, or you'll have leakage. Use the tines of the fork to poke vents on top of each empanada (flour the fork, if it's sticking). Transfer the empanadas to the baking sheets and chill them uncovered for 20 minutes (or up to 8 hours).

BAKE THE EMPANADAS AND SERVE: Preheat the oven to 400°F (205°C). Brush the tops of the empanadas with the egg wash. Bake until they are golden, 12 to 14 minutes (rotate the pans in the oven halfway through baking, back to front and top to bottom, to ensure that all of the empanadas bake evenly). Transfer the empanadas to cooling racks. Serve them warm or at room temperature.

NOTES: This is sticky dough. For easier rolling, roll the pastry on a generously floured surface, flour the top of the pastry, and use a piece of plastic wrap (or parchment paper) directly over the top of the pastry so that the rolling pin doesn't stick. If you need to re-roll the dough, brush excess flour off the scraps with a clean pastry brush, and gather up the scraps; wrap them in plastic and chill them for 10 minutes.

To freeze the unbaked empanadas, do not brush the tops with egg wash. Place them in one layer on the prepared baking sheets and freeze them until solid. Transfer them to freezer-safe containers and keep them frozen for up to 3 months. To reheat, brush the tops of the frozen empanadas with the egg wash. Bake them directly from the freezer, adding 1 to 2 more minutes to the baking time.

BANANA PASTRIES COATED WITH SUGAR AND CINNAMON

++

★ PASTÉIS DE BANANA ★ BRAZIL ★

These crispy pillows, stuffed with bananas and bejeweled with sugar, make a scrumptious dessert any day of the week. They're sweet, but not too sweet. My neighbor Janine told me that her mother made these for her when she was a little girl. Like any fried dough, *pastéis* are good to eat all by themselves, but I love to serve them with a scoop of vanilla or dulce de leche ice cream. Bananas that are past their prime mash easily and work great in this recipe. The dough takes some time to master, but if you use egg roll wrappers instead, these are easy to whip together on the spur of the moment. However; the blistery texture of the *pastéis* dough makes them particularly crispy and flaky; thus, I find it's worth spending the time making the dough yourself. Plus, frozen, uncooked *pastéis* can be fried to order whenever you're craving them. For this reason, I make several batches of dough at a time. With a little planning, one afternoon in the kitchen can bring you innumerable moments of sweet bliss.

1 recipe *Pastéis* Dough (page 33)

4 large bananas, mashed

¼ cup (50 g) sugar

1 teaspoon ground cinnamon

Vegetable oil for frying

+++

MAKES **12** *PASTÉIS*

ASSEMBLE THE *PASTÉIS*: Make the dough as directed on page 33 and let it rest, covered with plastic, for 20 minutes at room temperature.

Line a large baking sheet with parchment paper; set it aside. Divide the dough in half. Roll out the first half to ¹⁄₁₆ inch (2 mm) thick (like for pasta). Using a pastry cutter or very sharp knife, cut it into 5-by-6-inch (12-by-15-cm) rectangles. Re-roll the scraps together, wrap them in plastic, and allow them to rest for 20 minutes. In the meantime, repeat with the other half of the dough, cutting and re-rolling the scraps (while allowing the dough to rest in between), until you have 12 rectangles.

Continued ➡

You may have to do this a third time, until all are cut. The bottom side of the rectangles will be sticky; the top should be dry.

Place the bananas on a large plate; set it aside. On a medium plate, combine the sugar and cinnamon; set it aside.

With a shorter side toward you, and the sticky side facing up, place 2 tablespoons of the bananas on the bottom half of each rectangle, leaving ½ inch (12 mm) all around. Fold the top over the filling and seal all of the sides well by pressing them together with your fingers. Crimp them shut with the tines of a fork. Transfer them to the prepared baking sheet.

FRY THE *PASTÉIS* AND SERVE: Fit a large baking sheet with a metal cooling rack; set it aside. In a large skillet with high sides, heat ½ to 1 inch (about 2 cm) of oil to 360°F (180°C) or use a deep-fryer according to the manufacturer's directions. Working in batches, carefully slide the *pastéis* into the oil. Fry them until they're puffy and golden, 1½ to 2 minutes, turning them over halfway through. If the oil gets too hot as you fry and they're browning too quickly, lower the temperature and let the oil cool slightly before frying any more. Remove them with a slotted spoon and place them on the prepared rack to drain. Let them cool for 1 minute before rolling them on all sides in the sugar mixture. Cool for 5 minutes before serving them.

NOTE: *Pastéis* are best fried immediately after shaping and eaten immediately after they're fried. Freeze them uncooked in a single layer; once solid, transfer them to freezer bags and keep them frozen for up to 3 months. Fry them without thawing (to prevent splatters) for 3 to 3½ minutes, or until they are golden and crispy; roll them in the cinnamon-sugar and serve.

GUAVA AND CREAM CHEESE PASTRIES

+++

★ PASTÉIS DE GUAVA E QUEIJO ★ BRAZIL ★

1 recipe *Pastéis* Dough (page 33)

12 tablespoons (170 g) guava paste

12 tablespoons (170 g) cream cheese

¼ cup (50 g) sugar

1 teaspoon ground cinnamon

Vegetable oil for frying

A little bit tangy and a little bit sweet, these empanadas are crispy, crunchy, and flaky all at the same time. Inside awaits one of the most classic flavor combinations in Latin American cuisines (a favorite from Cuba to Brazil)—guava and cream cheese. Guava paste is nectarous, chewy, and of a consistency similar to gummy candies. You'll find it sold in the Latin section of most supermarkets, packed in tins or in long boxes, or online (see Sources, page 172). Simply scoop out the amount you need into individual portions; save the rest and serve it with a cheese assortment. *Pastéis* such as these are favorites of my Brazilian friends and you'll understand why the moment you bite into one. Let them cool slightly before eating.

+++

MAKES **12** *PASTÉIS*

ASSEMBLE THE *PASTÉIS*: Make the dough as directed on page 33 and let it rest, covered with plastic, for 20 minutes at room temperature.

Line a large baking sheet with parchment paper; set it aside. Divide the dough in half. Roll out the first half to ¹⁄₁₆ inch (2 mm) thick (like for pasta). Using a pastry cutter or very sharp knife, cut it into 5-by-6-inch (12-by-15-cm) rectangles. Re-roll the scraps together, wrap them in plastic, and allow them to rest for 20 minutes. In the meantime, repeat with the other half of the dough, cutting and re-rolling the scraps (while allowing the dough to rest in between), until you have 12 rectangles. You may have to do this a third time, until all are cut. The bottom side of the rectangles will be sticky; the top should be dry.

Continued ➤

With a shorter side toward you, and the sticky side facing up, place 1 tablespoon of the guava paste and 1 tablespoon of the cream cheese on the bottom half of each rectangle, trying to spread them out a bit so they'll overlap, and leaving ½ inch (12 mm) all around. Fold the top over the filling and seal all of the sides well by pressing them together with your fingers. Crimp them shut with the tines of a fork. Transfer them to the prepared baking sheet.

FRY THE *PASTÉIS* AND SERVE: Fit a large baking sheet with a metal cooling rack; set it aside. On a medium plate, combine the sugar and cinnamon; set it aside. In a large skillet with high sides, heat ½ to 1 inch (about 2 cm) of oil to 360°F (180°C) or use a deep-fryer according to the manufacturer's directions. Working in batches, carefully slide the *pastéis* into the oil. Fry them until they're puffy and golden, 1½ to 2 minutes, turning them over halfway through. If the oil gets too hot as you fry and they're browning too quickly, lower the temperature and let the oil cool slightly before frying any more. Remove them with a slotted spoon and place them on the prepared rack to drain. Let them cool for 1 minute before rolling them on all sides in the sugar mixture. Let them cool for 5 minutes before serving.

NOTE: *Pastéis* are best eaten immediately after they're fried. Freeze them uncooked in a single layer; once solid, transfer them to freezer bags and keep them frozen for up to 3 months. Fry them without thawing (to prevent splatters) for 3 to 3½ minutes, or until they are golden and crispy; roll them in the cinnamon-sugar and serve.

JAM AND CREAM CHEESE MINI PIES

✦✦

★ EMPANADITAS DE MERMELADA Y QUESO CREMA ★
★ VARIOUS COUNTRIES ★

These small pastries offer a creamy and sweet filling that pleases the palate. When my girls were little, I'd keep the freezer stocked with small empanadas such as these that we could quickly bake and enjoy as an after-school snack. They're elegant enough for company and go well with a cup of coffee. Yet they're also great for when you find yourself alone in your kitchen with time to savor a cup of tea or hot cocoa. Use your favorite fruit jam or select tropical flavors such as guava, mango, or pineapple. Peanut butter is not a traditional Latin American spread, but feel free to substitute it for the cream cheese in this recipe, if you prefer.

1 recipe Flaky Dough (page 34)

10 tablespoons (140 g) cream cheese

⅓ cup (75 ml) fruit jam (any flavor)

Egg wash, made with 1 beaten egg and 2 teaspoons water

✦✦

MAKES 30 EMPANADAS

ASSEMBLE THE EMPANADAS: Make the dough as directed on page 34 and let it rest, covered with plastic, for at least 30 minutes or up to 48 hours in the refrigerator.

Line two large baking sheets with parchment paper. On a well-floured surface and with a well-floured rolling pin, roll out the pastry to about ⅛ inch (3 mm) thick (like for piecrust). Keep lightly dusting flour on your surface and rolling pin as you roll so that the pastry doesn't tear or stick (see Notes). Using a 3½-inch (9-cm) round cutter, make 30 discs, rolling and cutting the scraps as needed.

Place 1 teaspoon of the cream cheese and ½ teaspoon of the jam on the bottom half of each pastry round. Brush the edges of the rounds with the egg wash and fold them in half over the filling to form half-moons. Seal the edges of the empanadas

Continued ➤

very well with your fingers and crimp them shut tight with the tines of a fork. It's important to seal these empanadas very tightly, or you'll have leakage. Use the tines of the fork to poke vents on top of each empanada (flour the fork, if it's sticking). Transfer the empanadas to the prepared baking sheets. Chill them uncovered for 20 minutes (or up to 8 hours).

BAKE THE EMPANADAS AND SERVE: Preheat the oven to 400°F (205°C). Brush the tops of the empanadas with the egg wash. Bake until they are golden, 12 to 14 minutes (rotate the pans in the oven halfway through baking, back to front and top to bottom, to ensure that all of the empanadas bake evenly). Transfer the empanadas to cooling racks. Serve them warm or at room temperature.

NOTES: This is sticky dough. For easier rolling, roll the pastry on a generously floured surface, flour the top of the pastry, and place a piece of plastic wrap (or parchment paper) directly over the top of the pastry so that the rolling pin doesn't stick. If you need to re-roll the dough, brush excess flour off the scraps with a clean pastry brush, and gather up the scraps; wrap them in plastic and chill them for 10 minutes.

To freeze the unbaked empanadas, do not brush the tops with egg wash. Place them in one layer on the prepared baking sheets and freeze until solid. Transfer them to freezer-safe containers and keep them frozen for up to 4 months. To reheat, brush them with the egg wash and bake them directly from the freezer. Bake for 15 to 18 minutes, until their centers are hot.

★ CHAPTER 7 ★

SALSAS

SALSA MEANS "SAUCE" IN SPANISH. SOME SAUCES ARE RAW, AND OTHERS ARE COOKED. MOST EMPANADAS ARE MEANT TO BE ENJOYED WITHOUT ANY TOPPING, BUT LATIN AMERICANS USE SAUCES TO EMBELLISH CERTAIN KINDS OF EMPANADAS. In Argentina and Peru, for instance, many eateries offer ramekins filled to the brim with liquid accoutrements that customers can spoon over the empanadas as they bite off pieces. And in Mexico and Central America, empanadas will often be dipped into richly colored salsas. You'll find the selection of sauces in this chapter to be luscious and colorful. These will help you elevate empanadas to another level. They will enhance flavors and complement the different crusts that surround them. The beef empanadas from Argentina and Uruguay will pair beautifully with the chimichurri, while the masa-based empanadas will be best when drizzled with either the red sauce or green tomatillo sauce featured in this chapter. Chileans prefer their empanadas embellished with raw and chunky pepper-based salsas, while Peruvians tend to select zestier garnishes, so I offer them both here. Some of the sauces in this chapter are spicy, while others are nutty and tangy. Throughout the book, I offer you suggestions as to which sauces to pair with the empanadas, but you should feel free to experiment with them and use them as you wish. Any leftover sauces will be great draped over other foods too, such as grilled beef and seafood, and spooned over eggs.

KNIFE-CUT PARSLEY SAUCE

★ CHIMICHURRI AL CUCHILLO ★ ARGENTINA ★

1 cup (40 g) finely chopped fresh Italian parsley (leaves and tender stems)

⅓ cup (40 g) finely chopped white onion

4 large cloves garlic, minced

1½ tablespoons red wine vinegar

½ teaspoon fine sea salt

¼ teaspoon red pepper flakes

¼ teaspoon freshly ground black pepper

½ cup (120 ml) extra-virgin olive oil

There are many recipes for this famous Argentinean herb mélange called chimichurri. This one is said to be *al cuchillo* because the ingredients are quickly chopped with a knife and stirred together into a sauce. This is my condiment of choice for any of the empanadas made with beef or for any of those made with the Bread Dough (page 30). The fact that all of the ingredients are finely minced gives this sauce a toothsome texture.

MAKES 1 CUP (240 ML)

In a medium bowl, combine the parsley, onion, garlic, vinegar, salt, red pepper flakes, and black pepper. Whisk in the oil until combined. Cover and let the chimichurri sit at room temperature for 30 minutes before serving.

> **NOTE:** This sauce can keep, covered, in the refrigerator for up to 3 days. Bring it back to room temperature before serving.

MANGO AND
AVOCADO SALSA
(PAGE 168)

KNIFE-CUT
PARSLEY SAUCE
(OPPOSITE)

DRIED CHILE,
BELL PEPPER,
AND TOMATO
SAUCE (PAGE 169)

RAW TOMATILLO
SALSA (PAGE 171)

YELLOW PEPPER
AIOLI (PAGE 170)

RED PEPPER
SALSA (PAGE 164)

RED PEPPER SALSA

+++

★ PEBRE ★ CHILE ★

1 cup (120 g) finely minced white onions

½ cup (50 g) finely minced red bell pepper

4 large cloves garlic, finely minced

2 tablespoons Italian hot red pepper paste

¼ cup (60 ml) red wine vinegar

½ cup (120 ml) extra-virgin olive oil

1 teaspoon dried oregano

1½ teaspoons fine sea salt, or to taste

½ teaspoon freshly ground black pepper, or to taste

Pebre, the ubiquitous spicy salsa of Chile, gets its red color from chile paste and not from tomatoes. Most food historians agree that *pebre* most probably dates back to the Middle Ages, when a mixture of onions, garlic, and vinegar similar to this was used to season dishes in Spain. It's also believed that the Spaniards introduced it to Chile during the Latin American colonial period (early sixteenth century to the start of the eighteenth century). In the New World, peppers, which were native to the Americas, were added to the formula. There are many recipes for *pebre*. Some cooks add cilantro or parsley, while others add a touch of tomatoes. I'm partial to the clean flavors found in this recipe. It's a cinch to prepare and it is a scrumptious condiment for any of the beef empanadas in this book, particularly the Chilean Famous Beef, Raisin, and Olive Hand Pies (page 69). Bite the tip off an empanada and then spoon a small amount of this sauce into the filling. It's spicy, so a little will go a long way. Italian red pepper paste is sold in tubes in many grocery stores and gourmet centers.

+++

MAKES ABOUT 2 CUPS (480 ML)

In a medium bowl, stir together the onions, bell pepper, and garlic. In a small bowl, combine the red pepper paste and vinegar, stirring to dissolve the paste. Whisk in the oil until it has emulsified. Stir in the oregano and season with the salt and black pepper. Combine the contents of the two bowls. Cover and let the *pebre* sit at room temperature for 30 minutes before serving.

NOTE: This sauce can keep, covered, in the refrigerator for up to 2 days. Bring it back to room temperature before serving.

CREAMY PEANUT SAUCE WITH TOPPINGS

★ AJÍ DE MANÍ ★ COLOMBIA ★

This creamy and velvety peanut sauce looks a lot like hummus. It's traditionally topped with crunchy, colorful vegetables and it's a classic accompaniment for the Spicy Potato and Peanut Empanadas (page 38). This is one of the many recipes that showcases the African culinary influences that define the food of the Cauca region of Colombia. Try it also with the cassava empanadas in this book, such as the Fried Cassava and Cheese Turnovers (page 58). Leftovers are great spooned over steamed green beans, asparagus, and potatoes (it makes a great dressing for potato salad).

MAKES 2 CUPS (480 ML)

In a blender, combine the peanuts and broth; blend until a paste forms. Add the serrano pepper and the egg; blend again, until the sauce is thick and creamy. Transfer it to a medium bowl and stir in the salt and lemon juice, to taste. Cover and chill the sauce for at least 2 hours before serving. When ready to serve, sprinkle it with the onions, tomatoes, and cilantro.

> **NOTE:** This sauce can keep, covered, in the refrigerator for up to 3 days. Serve cold or at room temperature.

2 cups (300 g) roasted unsalted peanuts

1¼ cups (300 ml) chicken or vegetable broth

1 serrano pepper (seeded and deveined for less heat), finely minced

1 hard-boiled egg (see page 15), peeled and quartered

1 teaspoon fine sea salt, or to taste

¼ cup (60 ml) fresh lemon juice, or to taste

½ cup (50 g) finely sliced green onions (white and light green parts only)

½ cup (90 g) peeled, seeded, and finely chopped plum tomatoes

¼ cup (10 g) coarsely chopped fresh cilantro (leaves and tender stems)

CREAMY PEANUT
SAUCE WITH TOPPINGS
(PAGE 165)

AVOCADO SALSA
(OPPOSITE)

AVOCADO SALSA

★ GUASACACA ★ VENEZUELA ★

This is Venezuela's rendition of avocado salsa, and it's one of the most popular sauces to serve with the cornmeal-crusted empanadas in this book. It may look like guacamole, but the vinegar imparts a very different flavor profile. Caribbean sweet peppers (known as *ajíes dulces*) resemble habanero peppers, but without any of the fiery heat; substitute deveined and seeded serrano peppers, or with more bell pepper, if necessary. Try this sauce with the Cumin Shredded Beef Empanadas (page 81), or the Black Bean and Cheese "Domino" Pies (page 52).

+ +

MAKES ABOUT 1½ CUPS (360 ML)

Slice the avocados in half; remove the pits and discard them. With a spoon, scoop out the flesh of the avocados and place it in a medium bowl. Mash the avocado with the tines of a fork (it should still retain some chunks). Add the vinegar, green onion, red onion, bell pepper, tomato, parsley, *ají* or serrano pepper, salt, and black pepper. Stir well and serve it immediately.

> **NOTE:** This sauce can keep, covered, in the refrigerator for up to 2 hours. Serve cold or at room temperature

2 ripe Hass avocados

2 tablespoons red wine vinegar

1 green onion, thinly sliced (white and light green parts only)

2 tablespoons minced red onion

2 tablespoons minced red bell pepper

2 tablespoons seeded and minced plum tomato

2 tablespoons minced fresh Italian parsley (leaves and tender stems)

1 *ají dulce*, seeded and minced, or serrano pepper (seeded and deveined for less heat)

½ teaspoon fine sea salt, or to taste

¼ teaspoon freshly ground black pepper, or to taste

MANGO AND AVOCADO SALSA

★ GUASACACA DE MANGO ★ VENEZUELA ★

2 ripe Hass avocados

1 large, semi-ripe mango, peeled and finely chopped into cubes (see Notes)

2 tablespoons red wine vinegar

1 green onion, thinly sliced (white and light green parts only)

2 tablespoons minced red onion

2 tablespoons minced red bell pepper

2 tablespoons seeded and minced plum tomato

2 tablespoons minced fresh Italian parsley (leaves and tender stems)

2 tablespoons minced cilantro (leaves and tender stems)

1 *ají dulce*, seeded and minced, or serrano pepper (seeded and deveined for less heat)

½ teaspoon fine sea salt, or to taste

¼ teaspoon freshly ground black pepper, or to taste

This is another rendition of the Venezuelan sauce that often serves as an accoutrement to the corn-encrusted empanadas. This colorful version has a sweeter profile than one made strictly with avocado. I find it's also an excellent salsa to serve alongside any of the masa-based empanada recipes in this book. This salsa is particularly delicious when served with the Cumin Shredded Beef Empanadas (page 81) and with the Stewed Chicken and Annatto Corn Empanadas (page 119), and it makes a succulent topping for any of the cassava empanadas in this book. Leftovers can be served over grilled salmon or chicken.

MAKES ABOUT 2¼ CUPS (540 ML)

Slice the avocados in half; remove the pits and discard them. With a spoon, scoop out the flesh of the avocados and place it in a medium bowl. Mash the avocado with the tines of a fork (it should still retain some chunks). Add the mango, vinegar, green onion, red onion, bell pepper, tomato, parsley, cilantro, *ají* or serrano pepper, salt, and black pepper. Stir well and serve it immediately.

> **NOTES:** Select mangoes that barely yield to the touch. If the mango is too ripe, it will be difficult to cut and the pieces will not hold their shape. Peel mangoes with a serrated potato peeler or a sharp knife. With a sharp knife, slice off both ends of the mango so that it has flat surfaces on which to stand. The seed of the mango is a flat oval pit that runs through the center of the fruit. Stand the mango on one of its ends, and slice down one side as close to the seed as you possibly can. Do the same thing on the other side. Lay the seed flat on the cutting board and slice the pulp that remains on the sides of the seed. Chop the flesh of the mango as the recipe directs and discard the seed.
>
> This sauce can keep, covered, in the refrigerator for up to 2 hours. Serve cold or at room temperature.

DRIED CHILE, BELL PEPPER, AND TOMATO SAUCE

++

★ SALSA ROJA ★ GUATEMALA, MEXICO ★

This thick and spicy sauce pairs beautifully with the masa-based empanadas in this book. The sauce is "fried" in oil, using a technique in which sauce is added to hot oil to seal in the flavor. This creates a luxurious, deep taste that cannot be otherwise obtained by simply simmering the sauce. Use a deep pot, a splatter guard, and a long spatula. The sauce should sizzle when it comes into contact with the oil. As the sauce thickens, it will splatter more enthusiastically and you will have to reduce the heat. Spoon any leftovers over fried eggs, or use it as a base for soups or stews.

++

MAKES ABOUT 2½ CUPS (600 ML)

Place the guajillo and ancho chiles in a medium bowl; cover them with boiling water. Place a heavy plate over them to keep them submerged; soak them for 15 minutes. Drain them; remove the stems and seeds and devein them. Place the chiles in a blender. Add the tomatoes, roasted bell peppers, onion, garlic, salt, cumin, and black pepper. Blend until the sauce is smooth.

Heat the oil in a medium Dutch oven set over medium-high heat, until it's shimmering. All at once, add the sauce (keep a distance from the pot as you do this because it will splatter), and stir it with a long wooden spatula. Immediately reduce the heat to medium-low, place a splatter guard on the pot, and cook the salsa for 3 minutes. Reduce the heat again to low; simmer it, uncovered, for 20 to 25 minutes, or until thickened, stirring the salsa occasionally. Serve it hot or at room temperature.

> **NOTE:** This sauce can keep, covered, in the refrigerator for up to 5 days or frozen for up to 3 months; simply reheat it when ready to use.

2 dried guajillo chiles

2 dried ancho chiles

Boiling water

1 (14½-ounce/415-g) can diced tomatoes with juices

2 large roasted red bell peppers (see page 15), seeded, cored, and deveined

½ cup (60 g) roughly chopped white onion

3 large cloves garlic, thinly sliced

1½ teaspoons fine sea salt

1 teaspoon ground cumin

½ teaspoon freshly ground black pepper

¼ cup (60 ml) vegetable oil

YELLOW PEPPER AIOLI

+++

★ SALSA CREMOSA DE AJí AMARILLO ★ PERU ★

1 cup (240 ml) mayonnaise

4 whole *ajíes amarillos*, peeled, seeded, and deveined

3 large cloves garlic, minced

1 tablespoon fresh lime juice, or to taste

¾ teaspoon fine sea salt, or to taste

¼ teaspoon ground cumin

Pinch of freshly ground black pepper

¼ cup (15 g) minced fresh chives (optional)

This pale yellow sauce is creamy, spicy, garlicky, and sour all at the same time. This is one of the condiments most commonly served with empanadas in Peruvian eateries. *Ajíes amarillos* are bright yellow peppers used in Peruvian cuisine. You'll find them packed in jars or cans in most Latin American stores; you can order them online (see Sources, page 172). Their flavor is spicy and fruity, and when preserved in brine, they're easy to peel. This aioli is a magnificent partner to any of the seafood empanadas in this book and I find that it also pairs well with beef empanadas. In the improbable case that you find yourself with leftovers, use it as a spread for sandwiches, as a sauce for fish and seafood, or as a dressing for potato salad.

++

MAKES 1¼ CUPS (300 ML)

In a blender, combine the mayonnaise, *ajíes*, garlic, lime juice, salt, cumin, and black pepper; blend until smooth. Transfer the salsa to a bowl; cover, and chill it for at least 1 hour before serving. Garnish it with the chives, if using.

> **NOTE:** This sauce can keep, covered, in the refrigerator for up to 4 days. Serve cold.

RAW TOMATILLO SALSA

This vibrantly green salsa is spicy, sour, and perfectly suited for the masa-encrusted empanadas in this book, such as the Cheese and Loroco Masa Pies (page 49), the Chorizo and Potato Pies (page 101), or the Crispy Cassava and Beef Empanadas (page 90). Tomatillos resemble tiny green tomatoes but are actually members of the gooseberry family. In Central America, they're known as *miltomates* (a thousand tomatoes) because the plant produces copious amounts of them at a time. To remove their papery husk, peel it off and rinse the tomatillos under cold running water to remove the gluey residue. Big tomatillos tend to be bitter, while smaller tomatillos are perfectly tangy. I suggest you use medium-sized tomatillos; four to five whole, medium tomatillos will yield 1 cup (185 g) chopped. Resist the temptation to seed the serrano peppers in this recipe, unless you're truly sensitive to the heat from the chiles.

+++

MAKES ABOUT 3 CUPS (720 ML)

In a blender, combine the tomatillos, cilantro, white onion, green onions, serrano peppers, garlic, honey, salt, and black pepper (and enough water to get the motor running, about ¼ cup/60 ml). Blend the ingredients on high speed until smooth. Chill the salsa, covered, for at least 30 minutes before serving.

> **NOTE:** This sauce can keep, covered, in the refrigerator for up to 3 days. Serve cold or at room temperature.

1 pound (455 g) tomatillos, husks removed, rinsed, and quartered

2 cups (80 g) packed fresh cilantro (leaves and tender stems)

½ cup (60 g) minced white onion

5 green onions, thinly sliced (white and light green parts only)

1 large or 2 medium serrano peppers (seeded and deveined for less heat), minced

2 large cloves garlic, roughly chopped

1 tablespoon honey

1 teaspoon fine sea salt, or to taste

½ teaspoon freshly ground black pepper, or to taste

SOURCES

✦✦

If you have difficulty finding any recipe ingredients or equipment in your local stores, it's easy to order products online or through a mail-order service. Here are a few of my favorites:

CRATE AND BARREL
www.crateandbarrel.com
Order tortilla presses, measuring cups and spoons, and baking and cooking utensils.

DEAN & DELUCA
www.deandeluca.com
With many locations around the country, it's a good place to find plenty of spices, herbs, ground chile powders, dulce de leche, Mexican oregano, and annatto seeds.

FRIEDA'S
www.friedas.com
Dried chiles (guajillo, ancho, de árbol, pasilla, etc.), plantains, pepitas (pumpkin seeds), and Mexican *canela* are on offer.

GOYA FOODS
www.goya.com
Find frozen empanada discs (for both frying and baking), loroco, salted cod and pollock, masarepa or P.A.N. arepa flour, frozen yuca, tapioca or yuca flour (called *almidón de yuca* or yuca harina), *ajíes amarillos* (whole and paste), refried black beans, capers, olives, annatto seeds and powders, chipotle chiles in adobo sauce, guava paste, and jelly.

LA FE
www.lafe.com
With three brick-and-mortar locations (Florida, North Carolina, and New Jersey), this can be a convenient source for prepared empanada discs, Mexican crema, and frozen yuca.

LA TIENDA
www.tienda.com
They specialize in products from Spain, but they have a great line called "New World" products that includes *ajíes amarillos* (whole and paste) and smoked paprika. They ship all over the U.S.

LODGE CAST IRON
www.lodgemfg.com
Their cast-iron skillets are excellent and are the ideal tool for charring vegetables and deep-frying. You can also find griddles.

MELISSA'S PRODUCE
www.melissas.com
Order dried chiles (such as ancho, guajillo, chipotle, de árbol, pasilla, etc.), Mexican *canela*, vanilla beans, pepitas (pumpkin seeds), *piloncillo* (or *panela*), and fresh yuca root.

MEX GROCER
www.mexgrocer.com
Order tortilla presses, Bijol, annatto, dried chiles (whole and ground), masa harina, Mexican cheese, and crema.

PENZEY'S SPICES
www.penzeys.com
This handy mail-order shop has loads of spices: annatto seeds, cayenne pepper, Mexican *canela* (they call theirs "Ceylon soft-stick cinnamon"), Mexican oregano, chipotle, ancho, guajillo peppers (whole and ground), coriander, and cumin. They also carry vanilla and almond extracts.

SUR LA TABLE
www.surlatable.com
Look for tortilla presses and all sorts of cooking and baking utensils.

WILLIAMS–SONOMA
www.williams-sonoma.com
Get tortilla presses, food scales, measuring cups and spoons, rolling pins, cookware, cooking thermometers, etc.

INDEX

✦✦

Page numbers in *italics* refer to photographs.

A

achiote (annatto), *16*, 40
   chicken empanadas with, 119–21, *120*
ají de maní, 165, 166
ajíes amarillos (yellow peppers)
   chicken empanadas with, 116–18, *117*
   sauce, *163*, 170
ajíes cachuchas (peppers), *13*
apple and caramel empanadas, 144–45, *146–47*
Avocado Salsa, *166*, 167
   with mango, *163*, 168

B

baking sheets, 12
Banana Pastries Coated with Sugar and Cinnamon, 151–53, *152*
beans, refried, 15
beef
   empanadas with. *see* beef empanadas
   flank steak, cooking, 18
Beef and Dried Chile Masa Pies, 78–80, *79*
beef empanadas
   cassava and, 90–92, *91*
   dried chiles and, 78–80, *79*
   egg, green onion and, 66–68, *67*
   ground, herbs and, 87–89, *88*
   plantain and, 75–77, *76*
   potato and, 72–74, *73*
   raisin, olive and, 69–71, *70*
   shredded, cumin and, 81–83, *82*
   stir-fried, onions, peppers and, 84–86, *85*
beef tallow, rendering, 14
Black Bean and Cheese "Domino" Pies, 52–54, *53*
blender, 13
Bread Dough, *23*, 30
butter, unsalted, 14

C

Candied Pineapple Pies, 148–50, *149*
Caramel-Apple Pies, 144–45, *146–47*
cassava (yuca)
   about, 15

beef empanadas with, 90–92, *91*
empanadas, with cheese, 58–60, *59*
Cassava or Yuca Dough, 28
   with cornmeal, 27
cast-iron skillet, *10*, 12
cativias, 90–92, *91*
Cheese and Loroco Masa Pies, 49–51, *50*
cheese empanadas
   black beans and, 52–54, *53*
   cassava and, fried, 58–60, *59*
   onion and, 61–63, *62*
Cheesy Spinach Empanadas, 41–43, *42*
chicken, poached, 19
chicken empanadas
   with annatto, 119–21, *120*
   green tomatillos and, 122–24, *123*
   mushrooms and, 106–7, *108–9*
   potatoes, green peas and, 125–27, *126*
   red peppers, olives and, 113–15, *114*
Chicken Masa Pies with Lettuce and Radishes, 110–12, *111*
Chicken Pies with Pecan and Yellow Pepper Sauce, 116–18, *117*
chile(s)
   beef empanadas with, 78–80, *79*
   salsa, with bell pepper, tomato sauce, *163*, 169
   types of, *16*
chimichurri al cuchillo, 162, *163*
Chorizo and Potato Pies with Tomatillo Salsa, 101–3, *102*
cilantro, *13*
cinnamon, banana pastries with, 151–53, *152*
Classic Ham and Cheese Pockets, 98–100, *99*
Cod and Potato Turnovers with Stewed Tomatoes and Olives, 139–41, *140*
Cooked Flank Steak, 18
cookie cutters, round, *10*, 12–13
cooking equipment, *10*, 11–13
cooling racks, 12
Corn and Spanish Smoked Paprika Turnovers, 44–45, *47*
corn flour, 13–14. *see also* masa harina; masarepa
Cornmeal and Cassava Dough, 27

Cornmeal Dough, *25*, 26
cream cheese
   about, 14
   fruit jam and, pastries, 157–59, *158*
   guava and, pastries, 154–56, *155*
Creamy Chicken and Mushroom Empanadas, 106–7, *108–9*
Creamy Peanut Sauce with Toppings, 165, *166*
Creamy Tuna and Roasted Red Pepper Pies, 133–35, *134*
Crispy Cassava and Beef Empanadas, 90–92, *91*
crust
   doughs for. *see* dough(s)
   store-bought frozen, 15
Cumin Shredded Beef Empanadas, 81–83, *82*

D

deep-fat frying, 12
deep-fat thermometer, 12
dobladas
   de jocón, 122–24, *123*
   de loroco, 49–51, *50*
   de pollo, 110–12, *113*
"Domino" Pies (Black Bean and Cheese), 52–54, *53*
dough(s)
   bread, *23*, 30
   cassava or yuca, 28
   cornmeal, 26
   cornmeal and cassava, 27
   flaky, *23*, 34
   gluten-free. *see* gluten-free doughs
   masa, 24, *25*
   master, *23*, 29
   mixing/matching, 22
   pastéis, 33
   plantain, 35
   repulgue method for, 31
   rolling out, 22
   salteña, *23*, 32
Dried Chile, Bell Pepper, and Tomato Sauce, *163*, 169
Dutch oven, 12

E

eggs
  beef, green onion empanadas with, 66–68, *67*
  egg wash, 30
  hard-boiled, 15
empanadas
  de ají de gallina, 116–18, *117*
  de atún, 136–38, *137*
  de atún y morrones, 133–35, *134*
  de carne mechada, 81–83, *82*
  de carne y salsa de chiles, 78–80, *79*
  de cerdo, 93–94, *95*
  de cuaresma, 139–141, *140*
  de dulce de piña, 148–150, *149*
  de espinaca y queso, 41–43, *42*
  de guiso de pollo, 119–121, *120*
  de lomo saltado, 84–86, *85*
  de maduros y picadillo, 75–77, *76*
  de manzana y dulce de leche, 144–45, *146–47*
  de papa y chorizo, 101–3, *102*
  de pollo y hongos, 106–7, *108–9*
  de pino, 69–71, *70*
  de pipián, 38–40, *39*
  de viento, 61–63, *62*
  de yuca y queso, 58–60, *59*
  with beef. *see* beef empanadas
  with chicken. *see* chicken empanadas
  continuing evolution of, 8–9
  dominó, 52–54, *53*
  doughs for. *see* dough(s)
  early history of, 5–6
  equipment for making, 11–13
  homemade versus storebought, 8
  ingredients for, 13–15
  Latin America and, 9
  modern-day, 6
  with pork. *see* pork empanadas
  portability of, 5
  sauces for. *see* salsa
  tucumanas, 66–68, *67*
  with tuna, 133–38
  variety of fillings/flavors, 6–7
empanaditas
  de choclo, 44–45, *47*
  de jamón y queso, 98–100, *99*
  de mermelada y queso crema, 157–59, *158*
  de queso y nueces, 46–48, *47*
equipment, cooking, *10*, 11–13

F

Famous Beef, Raisin, and Olive Hand Pies, 69–71, *70*

fillings, for empanadas. *see also specific recipes*
  flank steak, 18
  making/using, 17
  poached chicken, 19
Flaky Dough, *23*, 34
Flaky Ground Beef and Herb Pillows, 87–89, *88*
Flaky Hearts of Palm Pillows, 55–57, *56*
flank steak, cooked, 18
flour
  all-purpose unbleached, 13
  corn, 13–14. *see also* masa harina; masarepa
food processor, 13
freezer bags, zip-top plastic, 11, 22
Fried Cassava and Cheese Turnovers, 58–60, *59*

G

garlic, *16*
gluten-free
  dough substitutions, 22
  recipes
    Cassava or Yuca Dough, 28
    Cornmeal Dough, 26
    Cornmeal and Cassava Dough, 27
    Masa Dough, 24, *25*
    Plantain Dough, 35
Golden and Juicy Beef and Potato Pies, 72–74, *73*
Golden Chicken, Potato, and Green Pea Pies, 125–27, *126*
green peas, chicken empanadas with, 125–27, *126*
Green Tomatillo Chicken Stew Empanadas, 122–24, *123*
griddle, 12
grilled empanadas, 101–3, 122–24
guasacaca, *166*, 167
guasacaca de mango, *163*, 168
Guava and Cream Cheese Pastries, 154–56, *155*

H

half-sheet pans, 12
ham and cheese empanadas, 98–100, *99*
Hand-Cut Beef, Egg, and Green Onion Empanadas, 66–68, *67*
harina pan
  about, 14
  cassava and, dough, 27
  dough, *25*, 26
  working with, 25
hearts of palm *pastéis*, 55–57, *56*
honey, *16*

I

ingredients, for empanadas, 13

J

jalapeño pepper and tuna empanadas, 136–38, *137*
Jam and Cream Cheese Mini Pies, 157–59, *158*

K

kitchen scale, 11
kitchen scissors, *10*, 11
Knife-Cut Parsley Sauce, 162, *163*

L

lard, pork, rendering of, 14
lettuce, shredded, chicken empanadas with, 110–12, *111*
Light-As-Air Onion and Cheese Pies, 61–63, *62*
loroco
  cheese and, empanadas, 49–51, *50*
  flower buds, *16*

M

mango, 15
Mango and Avocado Salsa, *163*, 168
Maria José's Tuna, Jalapeño, and Tomato Turnovers, 136–38, *137*
Masa Dough, 24, *25*
  cheese and loroco pies with, 49–51, *50*
masa harina
  about, 13–14
  working with, 25
masarepa
  about, 14
  casava and, dough, 27
  dough, *25*, 26
  working with, 25
Master Dough, *23*, 29
measuring cups, *10*, 13
measuring spoons, *10*, 13
membrillo, *16*
Mexican oregano, *16*

O

olives
  beef, raisin empanadas with, 69–71, *70*
  chicken, red pepper empanadas with, 113–15, *114*
  cod, potato empanadas with, 139–41, *140*
onions
  beef, egg empanadas with, 66–68, *67*
  beef, red pepper empanadas with, 84–86, *85*

cheese empanadas with, 61–63, *62*
oregano, Mexican, *16*

P

pans, half-sheet, 12
paprika and corn turnovers, 44–45, *47*
parchment paper, *10*, 12
parsley sauce, 162, *163*
pastéis
    de banana, 151–153, *152*
    de camarão, 130–32, *131*
    de carne moida, 87–89, *88*
    de palmito, 55–57, *56*
    de guava e queijo, 154–56, *155*
    dough, 33
pastelitos
    de cerdo, *95*, 96–97
    de pollo, 113–115, *114*
pastry cutter, *10*, 13
peanut(s)
    potato empanadas with, 38–40, *39*
    sauce with toppings, 165, *166*
pebre, *163*, 164
pecans, chicken empanadas with, 116–18,
    117
peppers
    chile. *see* chile(s)
    red. *see* red pepper(s)
    roasted, 15
    types of, *13*
pineapple, candied, empanadas, 148–50,
    149
plantain, *15*
    beef empanadas with, 75–77, *76*
    dough, 35
plastic freezer bags, 11, 22
Poached Chicken, 19
pork empanadas
    chorizo, potato and, 101–3, *102*
    ham, cheese and, 98–100, *99*
    raisins and, 93–94, *95*
    sweet and savory, *95*, 96–97
pork lard, rendering, 14
potato(es)
    beef empanadas with, 72–74, *73*
    chicken empanadas with, 125–27, *126*
    chorizo and, empanadas, 101–3, *102*
    cod and, empanadas, 139–41, *140*
    peanut and, empanadas, 38–40, *39*

R

radishes, chicken empanadas with, 110–12,
    111
raisin, beef, and olive empanadas, 69–71, *70*
Ravioli-Shaped Pies with Stir-Fried Beef,
    Onions, and Peppers, 84–86, *85*

Raw Tomatillo Salsa, *163*, 171
red pepper(s)
    beef, onion empanadas with, 84–86, *85*
    chicken, olive empanadas with, 113–15,
        114
    roasted, 15
    salsa, with dried chiles, tomato sauce,
        163, 169
    tuna empanadas with, 133–35, *134*
Red Pepper Salsa, *163*, 164
refried beans, canned, 15
repulgue method, for sealing, 31
    recipes using, 41–43, 66–68, 116–18,
        139–41
rolling pin, *10*, 13, 22
Roquefort and Walnut Mini Pies, 46–48, *47*
ruler, *10*, 11

S

salsa
    avocado, *166*, 167
    chile, red pepper and tomato, *163*, 169
    cremosa de ají amarillo, *163*, 170
    cruda de miltomates, *163*, 171
    mango and avocado, *163*, 168
    parsley, 162, *163*
    peanut, 165, *166*
    raw tomatillo, *163*, 171
    red pepper, *163*, 164
    roja, *163*, 169
    yellow pepper, *163*, 170
salt, fine sea, 14
salteñas
    de carne, 72–74, *75*
    de pollo, 125–27, *126*
    dough, 32
scale, kitchen, 11
scissors, kitchen, *10*, 11
Shrimp and Tomato Stew Flaky Pillows,
    130–32, *131*
skillet, cast-iron, *10*, 12
Spanish paprika and corn turnovers, 44–45,
    47
Spicy Potato and Peanut Empanadas,
    38–40, *39*
spinach empanadas, cheesy, *42*
spoons, measuring, *10*, 13
steak, cooked flank, 18
Stewed Chicken and Annatto Corn
    Empanadas, 119–21, *120*
stock, chicken, 19
Sugar-Coated Pork and Raisin Turnovers,
    93–94, *95*
Sweet and Savory Chicken, Roasted Red
    Pepper and Olive Pies, 113–15, *114*
Sweet and Savory Pork Pies, *95*, 96–97

Sweet Plantain and Beef Turnovers, 75–77,
    76
Sweet Plantain Dough, 35

T

tallow, beef, 14
thermometer, deep-fat, 12
tomatillo(s), *13*
    chicken empanadas with, 122–24, *123*
    raw, salsa, *163*, 171
tomato(es)
    stew, shrimp empanadas with, 130–32,
        131
    stewed, cod, potato empanadas with,
        139–41, *140*
    tuna empanadas with, 136–38, *137*
tortilla press
    about, *10*, 11
    method, 22
    recipes using, 27, 28, 38–40, 41–43,
        49–51, 52–54, 58–60, 66–68, 69–71,
        75–77, 78–80, 81–83, 84–86, 90–92,
        101–3, 110–12, 116–18, 119–12,
        122–24, 125–27, 136–38, 139–141
tuna empanadas
    jalapeño peppers, tomatoes with,
        136–38, *137*
    roasted red peppers with, 133–35, *134*

V

vegan
    dough substitutions, 22
    recipes, 24, 26, 27, 28, 35, 38–40, 162,
        164, 167, 168, 169, 171
vegetarian recipes, 24, 26, 27, 28, 34, 35,
    38–40, 41–43, 44–45, 46–48, 49–51,
    55–57, 58–60, 61–63, 144–45, 148–150,
    151–53, 154–156, 157–59, 162, 164,
    165, 167, 168, 169, 170, 171

W

walnut and Roquefort cheese mini pies,
    46–48, *47*

Y

Yellow Pepper Aioli, *163*, 170
yuca. *see* cassava (yuca)

Z

zip-top plastic freezer bags, 11, 22

ACKNOWLEDGMENTS

To everyone at Abrams and Stewart, Tabori & Chang: My sincere thanks go to Holly Dolce, for believing in this project from the start. Infinite gratitude goes to my fabulous editor, Laura Dozier, for her enthusiasm for the book and for making this a most beautiful and seamless process for me. Thank you, Sally Knapp and Denise LaCongo, for your great help with the production of this book. I'm thankful also to Ann Martin Rolke for her careful copyediting and to Kate Lesko and her entire marketing team for all they have done to support my work.

Pictures speak a thousand words, and I have the dream team to thank here: Thank you, Tina Rupp, for capturing the spirit of this book through your gorgeous photographs; to Penelope Bouklas, for selecting the most beautiful props to showcase my empanadas; and to Toni Brogan, for your careful food styling as you re-created each authentic empanada beautifully. My thanks go to designer Danielle Young and creative director John Gall, who designed a book that celebrates Latin American culture in such a colorful manner and who sought inspiration outside the box, in order to keep it fun.

My gratitude goes to my agent extraordinaire, my friend Lisa Ekus, for finding a home for this project and for suggesting I write this book. My thanks to Leslie Jonath, without whom the idea for this book would not have been possible.

I'm so very grateful to my recipe testers, led by my friend and professional recipe tester Liz Tarpy, who kept me in check with her impeccable attention to detail. Also, thanks to my friends Kim Callaway, Linda Christiana, Sally Ekus, Karin Fitzpatrick, and Athina Sgambati for re-testing all of the recipes with unending enthusiasm.

Thanks to Mark Kelly, who set me up with a collection of Lodge cast-iron skillets so that I could test my recipes. My deep gratitude goes to my friend and colleague Maricel Presilla, who inspires me to write about the authentic cuisines of our beloved Latin America; and to my friend Norman Van Aken, for believing in my work and for leading the pack, starting the love affair for Latin flavors in the U.S. that has made it possible for me to write about authentic Latin food in this country today.

To my beloved husband, Luis, and our daughters, Alessandra and Niccolle: Thank you for always encouraging me to write and for perpetuating our love for long *sobremesas* ("after-dinner talks") at our family table.

My humble gratitude to God, for blessings received.

Published in 2015 by Stewart, Tabori & Chang
An imprint of ABRAMS

Text copyright © 2015 Sandra A. Gutierrez
Photographs copyright © 2015 Tina Rupp

Library of Congress Control Number: 2014942973

ISBN: 978-1-61769-143-0

Editor: Laura Dozier
Designer: Danielle Young
Production Manager: Denise LaCongo

The text of this book was composed in CanCan de Bois, Champion, Helvetica Condensed, and Luchita Payol.

Printed and bound in the United States

10 9 8 7 6 5 4 3 2 1

Stewart, Tabori & Chang books are available at special discounts when purchased in quantity for premiums and promotions as well as fundraising or educational use. Special editions can also be created to specification. For details, contact specialsales@abramsbooks.com or the address below.

THE ART OF BOOKS SINCE 1949
115 West 18th Street
New York, NY 10011
www.abramsbooks.com